THE GREAT
FISH
— AND —
SEAFOOD
COOKBOOK

INTRODUCED BY BEVERLEY PIPER
RECIPES COMPILED BY JUDITH FERGUSON
PHOTOGRAPHED BY PETER BARRY
EDITED BY JILLIAN STEWART
DESIGNED BY CLAIRE LEIGHTON

This edition published in 1998 by Colour Library Direct
CLB 2615
© 1992 CLB International, a division of Quadrillion Publishing Ltd,
Godalming, Surrey, UK
All rights reserved
Printed and bound in Singapore
ISBN 1-85833-204-4

THE GREAT
FISH
— AND —
SEAFOOD
COOKBOOK

JUDITH FERGUSON

Colour
Library
Direct

CONTENTS

INTRODUCTION

The British adore seafood, and are eating more and more of it every year. Seafood evokes memories of shrimping, crabbing and watching fishermen return with their catches. It is these happy memories which contribute to many people's love of seafood. What other valuable food is available in such variety?

Nothing tastes quite like fresh seafood, it is naturally tender and will only toughen if overcooked. There is such a tremendous variety of seafood available that it makes sense to learn more about this crucial source of nutrients, and how it can best be incorporated into a diet which will please the whole family.

Fish is a wonderful food which is high in body building proteins and low in calories. White fish contains practically no fat, whilst oily fish varies in fat content from 0.5% - 20% and contains the sort of fatty acids which doctors believe may actually assist in preventing coronary heart disease.

Fish also contains almost no carbohydrate and is an excellent source of vitamins, and oily fish is particularly high in the fat soluble vitamins A and D, thiamin and riboflavin.

With all these important benefits to boast of, it is obvious why more use should be made of this easy-to-obtain food which is both delicious and nutritious. Sadly, many people have misconceptions about fish and shellfish, believing it is difficult to prepare and cook. This is just not true, follow the instructions given in the following pages and the different methods of preparing and cooking will become surprisingly simple.

One of the most common complaints about fish is that it smells. A famous chef once said 'Fish should smell like the tide. Once they smell like fish, it's too late'. So make sure when you buy fish that it has a wonderful 'straight from the shore' aroma and is moist and fresh.

CHOOSING FISH

This selection of popular shellfish (left) includes: a hard-shell crab (top left); a cooked lobster (top right); oysters, which can be purchased in the shell or shucked (second row, left); a soft shell or blue crab is one which sheds its shell (second row, middle); mussels are purchased in the shell; scallops (third row, left) are freshest when purchased in the shell; clams (third row middle) can be puchased with or without their shells; prawns can be bought in many different ways, uncooked (third row, right), cooked, without heads and whole; squid (bottom right) can be bought fresh or frozen.

Fish is often classified in different ways - firstly according to the type of flesh:-

White Fish has a distinctive white flesh and includes such favourites as cod, sole and sea bass.

Oily Fish has oil distributed through its flesh, giving it a grey or red tinge. This group includes trout, mackerel and sardines.

Shellfish is the group enclosed in a shell and is further classified into two groups - crustaceans usually have limbs and a shell, such as crabs and lobster, whilst molluscs e.g.. mussels, oysters etc. have a shell only.

Fish are also classified into groups determined by their shape:-

Round Fish have a rounded body with eyes at either side of the head and always swim dorsal fin up. This a very large group which includes a whole range of fish from freshwater salmon to sharks.

Flat Fish have both eyes on the top of their head, they swim on their sides, and are quick and easy to cook. This group includes skate and flounder.

Fish can be bought in a whole manner of shapes, sizes and cuts. Above is a small selection including clockwise: a whole flat fish, a cleaned round fish, a cleaned fish with head and tail removed, a fish steak, chunks of white fish, an unskinned butterflied steak, skinned fillets, unskinned fillets, and a whole round fish.

Buying Fish

When selecting fresh fish for the table it is important to choose the freshest fish possible. It is advantageous to buy a whole fish as it is very often cheaper than prepared cuts and is easier to judge for freshness. It should look moist and fresh, the eyes should be bright, the flesh firm, the gills red, the scales should sparkle and there should definitely be no unpleasant odour! Some fish have a natural slime which is easily removed by rinsing so don't be put off by it. If it is not possible or desirable to buy a whole fish, use the same guidelines when you select fish fillets or steaks. The flesh should look moist, bright, and white fish should be really white.

If possible fish should be used on the day of purchase, but if it must be stored it should be cleaned, washed and kept in the refrigerator overnight in a sealed container. Shellfish deteriorate rapidly and should always be bought for immediate use.

You will find a wide variety of fish and seafood at your local fishmonger, all of which you can buy ready prepared or whole. Cleaning and preparing fish is not at all difficult, just follow the step-by-step photographs and you will be surprised at how quickly you can have your fish ready for cooking.

Frozen Fish

Fresh fish is seasonal but frozen fish is, of course, available all year round. It is an excellent way to buy fish as only the very best quality fish is frozen and it is frozen as soon as it is caught to preserve the freshness. Frozen fish is almost always prepared for cooking before freezing, making it particularly easy for the cook to handle.

White fish may be stored in a domestic freezer for up to four months, whereas oily fish, because of its high fat content, is best consumed within three months. Shellfish, particularly prawns, should be consumed within two months of being frozen. Home-made fish dishes also freeze well, but should also not be stored for longer than two months. For the best results defrost frozen fish overnight in the refrigerator.

Canned Fish

Canned fish is a wonderful store cupboard standby which keeps fresh more or less indefinitely and is therefore valuable for outdoor enthusiasts and the like, as well as for convenience meals when unexpected guests arrive. Oily fish is particularly suitable for canning and is useful in a large number of recipes.

Smoked Fish

Smoking is a method of preserving fish which results in its characteristic smoky flavour – kippers is probably one of the best known smoked fish available, however smoked mackerel is also becoming more widely available and is often served as a starter. Becoming ever more popular is smoked salmon, which is prepared by cleaning and filleting the fresh fish, then smoking the fillets in a cold smoker often over apple chips and oak sawdust. The resulting smoked salmon has a strong colour, translucent appearance and tastes wonderful!

Food Value Fish

Nutritionally speaking, fish is one of the most valuable foods available to man. It is an excellent source of protein, which is needed for the growth and repair of body cells. It is also low in carbohydrates and saturated fats. Oily fish is rich in the fat-soluble vitamins A and D and all fish is rich in thiamin, riboflavin, niacin, B6, B12 pantothenic acid and biotin. Fish is also an excellent source of minerals, which are vitally necessary for the body's growth and functioning. Some of the smaller varieties of fish which are eaten whole, bones and all, provide a useful amount of calcium.

Fish is also fairly low in calories, especially when compared with other valuable protein foods such as meat and cheese. The approximate calorie counts below indicate just how useful fish is in a healthy diet:-

1oz of cod, steamed or poached in water	24 calories
1oz raw, ground beef	55 calories
1oz of leg of pork	72 calories
1oz Cheddar cheese	102 calories
1oz tuna in brine, canned	32 calories

Fish is quite rightly making a comeback – it is readily available and very versatile. The versatility of fish extends to the ways in which it may be cooked, so try the methods on pages 16-20, always remembering never to overcook.

PREPARING FISH AND SEAFOOD

HOW TO SCALE AND FIN A ROUND FISH

1

Holding the fish firmly by the tail, scrape towards the head of the fish with a scaler or the blunt side of a knife.

2

Rinse the fish thoroughly under cold running water to remove any remaining scales and residue which may be clinging to the skin.

3

Trim the dorsal fin with a pair of scissors. To remove the whole fin, snip through most of the fin in the direction of the head and then pull.

CLEANING A ROUND FISH

1

Holding the body of the fish firmly, cut the head off just behind the gills. The head may be saved for use in fish stock or soup.

2

Cut down the underside of the fish to the tail and remove the innards, which should come out with ease.

3

Clean and remove any remaining residue by rinsing the fish thoroughly in cold running water.

FILLETING A ROUND FISH

1

Holding the fish firmly, cut along the backbone from just behind the head to the tail.

2

Cut across the fish and slide the knife between the ribs and the flesh.

3

Carefully lift the fillet away, taking care not to break up the flesh.

SKINNING A FLAT FISH

Dip your fingers in salt to get a good grip then hold the fish by its tail and make a cut across the skin just above the tail.

Begin peeling the skin away from the cut. Pull the skin over the head, turn the fish over and pull the skin off of the underside.

1

2

SKINNING A FILLET

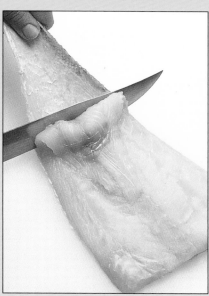

1

Get a firm grip on the tail end of the fillet, make a cut across the flesh and ease the fillet away from the skin in a sliding motion.

FILLETING A FLAT FISH

1

After skinning the fish, cut down, but not through, the backbone from behind the head to the tail.

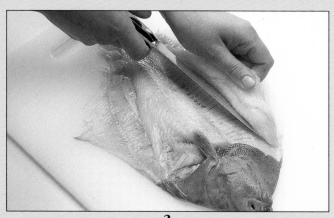

2

Insert the knife under the flesh at the top of the fish and cut down between the flesh and the bones until the fillet lifts off. Repeat on the other side.

OPENING OYSTERS

1

2

Hold the oyster tightly in one hand, and with the other, insert the oyster knife into the hinge, twisting until the shell opens.

Slide the blade under the oyster and cut through the connecting muscle to separate the oyster from its shell.

PREPARING MUSSELS

1 Scrub the mussels to remove any sand or barnacles.

Debeard the mussels by pulling the byssus which protrudes from the shell.

2

REMOVING MEAT FROM HARD-SHELL CRAB

1

Hold the crab firmly, twist apron flap and gently pull, removing the intestinal vein which is attached to the apron.

4

Crack the crab in two and remove any meat left on the central body section.

6

Scoop out the soft brown meat from the crab shell.

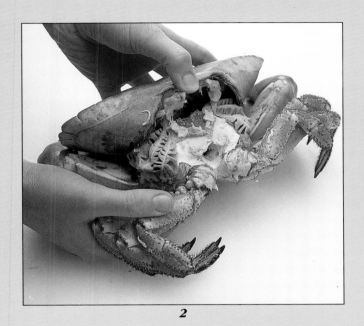

2

Holding the crab firmly with one hand, gently prise the shell off and put to one side for later use.

3

Remove the gills or "dead men's fingers" and discard.

5

Crack open the legs and extract the leg meat with a crab pick.

7

If using the shell to serve the meat, break of the rough edges and cut to form a neat edge.

8

The crab meat is now ready to be used in a recipe or can be served in the shell.

PREPARING LOBSTER

1

Using a sharp knife, cut the lobster down the centre, beginning behind the head.

2

Cut right through the lobster from head to tail to separate in two.

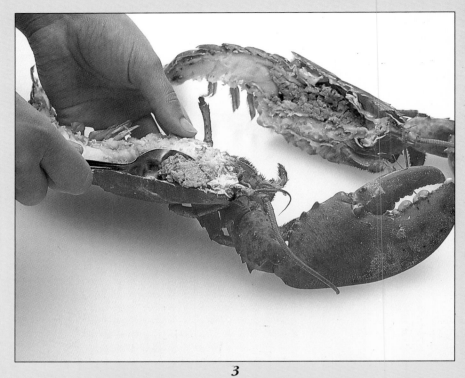

3

Remove the tomalley (green liver) from the lobster.

PREPARING PRAWNS

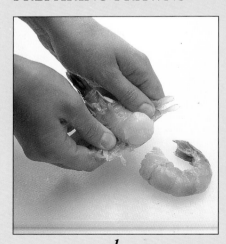

1

Remove the legs of the prawn and break off the shell by bending both sides backwards.

2

Cut down the back of the prawn, cutting deep enough just to expose the intestinal vein which should then be removed.

PREPARING SQUID

1

Detach the tentacles and hard beak from the body of the squid by holding the tentacles and pulling gently.

4

Holding the body of the lobster, break the tail section away from the body.

5

Break the tail section apart and remove the meat.

6

Cut the large part of the claw away from the bits which do not contain any meat.

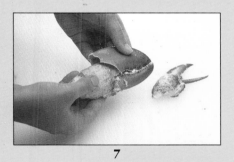

7

Crack the claws open to remove the meat.

8

The easiest way to remove the meat from the claws is with your fingers.

9

The meat from the shells should come out in one piece.

2

Remove the transparent quill and any remaining entrails by running your fingers along the body to the open end.

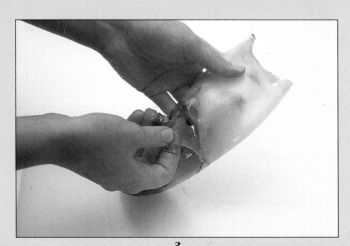

3

Peel off the skin by pulling from the cut end to the tail. The squid is now ready for use.

Microwave Cooking

The microwave oven is an excellent appliance to use for both defrosting and cooking fish. Timing is critical when microwaving fish and will differ according to the output of your particular model. A 700w microwave will cook faster than a 500w model. Remember also that the more you put into a microwave, the longer it will take to cook as the energy has to be shared between the amount of food in the cabinet. Standing time should also be considered, as food continues to cook for a short period after being removed from the microwave and this must be allowed for when cooking fish. It is always better to undercook as you can pop the fish back into the oven for a minute or two after the standing time has ended, but if you overcook the fish initially, it will be spoiled.

Rules for Microwaving Fish

1. Arrange fish in a single layer in a shallow dish. Always cover during cooking, unless using a browning dish to achieve a crisp finish. Covering will help keep the fish moist, will speed up cooking time, keep the flavour in the fish and help prevent the oven from becoming dirty.

2. Always cook foods in non-metallic containers, this includes those which have a metal rim or trim.

3. Whether your particular model has a turntable or not, always turn the fish over once during cooking.

4. When cooking fish steaks, arrange them in a ring fashion, keeping thicker parts towards the outside edge of the dish.

5. If the recipe calls for it, remember to stir as in a fish stew or soup – stirring, and turning where stirring is not advisable, are important parts of microwave cooking and help to ensure even cooking results.

6. Always cook fish for the minimum advised cooking time – it can always go back in the microwave after the standing time if necessary.

7. Fish benefits by the addition of a little liquid – add water, stock or lemon juice.

8. Do not add salt before microwaving as it tends to cause dryness.

Defrosting Fish

Frozen fish may be successfully defrosted using the defrost control on your microwave. Always lay the fish out in a single layer in a covered dish and turn over once half way through defrosting. Follow the chart in the manufacturer's manual, supplied with your oven so that you have a guide as to timings. Allow a standing time between defrosting and cooking as the fish will continue to defrost during this time, just as it continues to cook after the cooking time.

Fish can be cooked straight from frozen on 100% Full power in the microwave, although generally, it is easier to achieve perfect results if the fish is defrosted first. To cook straight through from frozen, simply double the cooking time given for cooking fresh fish, checking frequently and

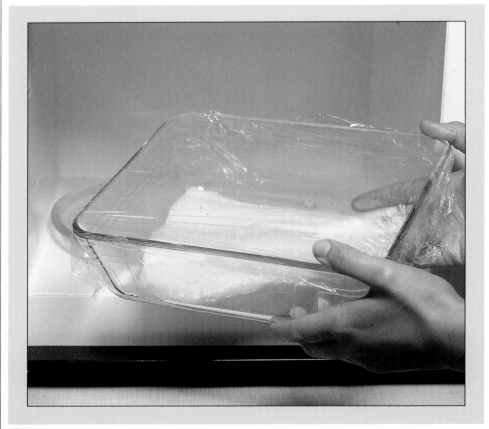

remembering to turn the fish during cooking and to allow a standing time at the end – 3 or 4 minutes standing is sufficient for most fish recipes.

Barbecuing

Barbecues are popular social occasions – there are very few people who do not enjoy a glass of wine and the aroma of food cooking on the open fire. As fish and seafood cooks quickly and easily, it is one of the best foods to cook by this method.

Remember that fish barbecues quickly, so take care to oil the barbecue grill rack and kebab sticks or fish grids and either marinade white fish or brush with oil before cooking. Add a little seasoning and some fresh herbs before cooking to impart a delicate flavour to the flesh of the fish.

Choose firm fish that will not disintegrate during cooking and cut into thick fillets or thick chunks for kebabs or barbecue whole fish with the cleaned belly filled with herbs. Make 2 or 3 slashes in the skin of whole fish before cooking and turn 2 or 3 times. Small whole fish will benefit from being wrapped in foil parcels before grilling. They will take about 30 minutes, so cook them arranged towards the edge of the barbecue, and add herbs such as thyme and rosemary, seasoning and a little lemon juice to the parcels before closing them.

For a delicious marinade, combine 240ml dry cider with 60ml walnut or olive oil, 1 clove crushed garlic, and 1 tablespoon mixed, crushed fresh herbs such as rosemary, thyme and marjoram.

Add ¼ teaspoon salt and a little finely ground black pepper. Mix well and pour over the fish. This amount of marinade will be sufficient for 6 people.

Braising

As fish cooks quickly it may seem slightly unusual to think of a fish casserole. However, it is a good moist method of cooking some of the less expensive cuts of fish. By this method large chunks of fish are cooked on top of a selection of chopped root vegetables which have been stir-fried in a little melted butter until softened and starting to brown. Liquid in the form of stock, wine, cider or apple juice to just cover the fish is added, with a little seasoning and some fresh herbs.

The pan is then covered with a lid and left over a gentle heat until the fish is tender. Serve the fish with the accompanying vegetables and liquid – thicken the sauce after lifting the fish if desired, but if you serve chunks of fresh bread with the stew your family or guests can simply soak the wonderful juices up with the bread.

Baking

This is an ideal method of cooking whole fish and also excellent for large fillets or steaks of fish. Baked fish should be cooked in a moderate oven preheated for 15 minutes. Prepared whole fish is delicious cooked on its own, simply seasoned and stuffed with a few herbs – remember to slash the skin in two or three places to ensure

over so that it is positioned at its lower level in the pan and then line it with foil before arranging the prepared fish onto the foil. This makes washing up much easier as the messy foil is simply screwed up and thrown away. The speed of cooking will vary according to your particular grill and how near the fish is to the intense heat. The fish will need turning once or twice during cooking and remember to test frequently to see if the fish is cooked.

Fish is best cooked under a medium heat which allows the heat to penetrate more evenly right through to the centre.

Deep-Fat Frying

Deep-fat frying is a fast method of cooking small whole fish such as whitebait. It is also a useful method of cooking small pieces of fish dipped in batter. The food is placed in a wire basket and lowered into a

even cooking. Lay in a shallow dish and bake uncovered for 45-60 minutes, according to size, and baste once or twice with the resulting fish juice. Fillets or steaks of fish will benefit by the addition of a little liquid in the form of stock or wine and should be covered with a lid or some foil. Be careful not to overcook the fish – test frequently and remove as soon as the flesh flakes easily. Allow roughly 6-10 minutes per pound plus 6-10 minutes over, according to the thickness of the fillets.

Whole fish cooked by this method makes an attractive centre piece for a buffet table and is often served cold, skinned and attractively garnished after cooking.

Grilling

This quick method of cooking is a popular way of dealing with fish

fillets, steaks, or small whole fish, such as anchovies.

The prepared fish should be seasoned and then brushed with a little oil. Try turning the grill rack

pan of oil which should come about ¾ of the way up the pan and be preheated to about 360°F. It is important that the oil is clean and of sufficient depth to cover the food. If the oil is not heated to sufficient temperature before the food is added, the resulting fish will be soggy, as the heat of the oil will not have immediately sealed the outside of the fish. However, if the oil is too hot, the outside of the food will burn before the inside has had time to cook.

Check the temperature of the oil with a cook's thermometer then you'll be sure of success!

As oil cooks food very quickly, fish, because of its very delicate nature, needs to have a protective coating added before it is exposed to the extreme temperature of the oil. The coating helps to stop the fish breaking up, and also acts as a flavour seal, locking the flavour into the food. Seasoned flour, batter or egg and breadcrumbs are all suitable coating for fish. Cook small quantities at a time so that the temperature of the oil is not reduced.

Once the fish is cooked (it will be golden and crisp) remove it immediately and drain on paper towels before serving with wedges of lemon.

Shallow Frying

Shallow frying is a quick method of cooking fairly small amounts of fillets, fish steaks and small whole fish such as herring and mackerel. The fish should be protected with some sort of coating – dipped in beaten egg and rolled in breadcrumbs is ideal or dipped in milk and then rolled in flour or

oatmeal. The oil should come just under half way up the pan and be heated until a shimmery haze rises from the pan. Add the fish and quickly seal on both sides then reduce heat slightly and cook until crisp and golden, turning once or twice. It is a good idea to cover the pan with a splatter guard to prevent splashing – this is a fine wire mesh cover with a heatproof handle designed to fit over the shallow frying pan completely during the frying process.

It prevents the fat splattering and is a definite advantage. Once the food is cooked it should be drained well on paper towels and served immediately.

Stir Frying

Stir frying is done in a large shallow frying pan, or ideally, in a wok. It is a useful method of cooking small pieces of fish or shellfish quickly.

Start by stir frying prepared vegetables such as onions and peppers in a little oil, then add the fish, which will cook in 30 seconds to 1 minute. An important factor in stir frying is that the ingredients are all assembled and prepared before the oil is heated. The vegetables should be cut into even-sized strips. The whole meal is cooked and served all from one pan and usually accompanied by boiled or fried rice. The food is simply cooked, by stirring continuously over a fairly high heat, using a slotted draining spoon. Soy sauce is often added before serving but there is a wide range of sauces, such as oyster sauce, which are very tasty.

Poaching

Poaching is cooking gently in a liquid such as wine, water, fish stock or milk. Heat the liquid first then add the fish – both whole fish,

fillets and fish cutlets are excellent cooked by this method. Cook them in a single layer, allowing the liquid to come about ¾ of the way up the fish. Season and cover with a tightly-fitting lid and poach small fillets and cutlets for about 8 minutes, whole fish may take 15-20 minutes.

Check continually, as when cooking fish by any other method and remove when the flesh in the thickest part of the fish flakes easily. The liquid should be used to make an accompanying sauce or reserved and used for a fish soup.

Steaming

Steaming is an easy method of cooking fish fillets which ensures the fish remains juicy as it is surrounded by moisture whilst cooking. Here again care should always be taken not to overcook. The fillet should be rolled or folded, lightly seasoned and steamed for 10-15 minutes in a steamer, covered with a closely fitted lid, over simmering water. If no steamer is available, steam the fish between 2 dinner plates over a pan of simmering water. Steamed

fish is full of flavour. Serve it on its own with freshly cooked vegetables in season, accompanied by a light parsley or cheese sauce, if required. The fish can also be steamed over water containing herbs to give a subtle flavour.

There's very little that can go wrong when steaming fish, simply ensure that there is sufficient water in the pan and that it is maintained at simmering point throughout the cooking process. Also, make sure that you cover the fish with a tightly-fitting lid, so that the steam which actually cooks the fish is kept in.

Fish Stock

A good basic fish stock can be made for almost nothing, using fish head, skin and bones supplied by your fishmonger. It is far quicker to make than meat stock, taking only 10-15 minutes and makes a delicately flavoured base for all types of sauces. To prepare the stock, put the fish heads, bones and skins into a large saucepan, and add a bouquet garnis with some seasoning. Cover bones etc. with cold water and simmer gently in the covered pan for 10-15 minutes. Strain and use as required.

Fish Soup

Fish soup deserves to be served more often. It is warming, nourishing and delicious. Fresh bread is all that is needed to turn fish soup into a filling and economical meal which is easy to prepare. Fish soups offer great scope for variety. Start with a simple recipe and then develop it using your own favourite ingredients.

Accompaniments for Fish

There is simply nothing to equal the flavour of fresh fish, well cooked and served with a garnish of fresh lemon and accompanied by a selection of fresh vegetables. However, there are many occasions when the addition of a well chosen sauce will greatly enhance a fish dish, so simply choose one of the following to serve with your favourite fish – your guests will be doubly impressed.

Coating Sauces

A coating sauce is made from a roux base and is designed to lightly coat the fish or vegetables with which it is to be served. It should be carefully prepared in a thick pan and served as soon as it is ready – a correctly made coating sauce should be of the consistency of thick cream and coat the back of a

wooden spoon. The sauce may be varied considerably according to the type of liquid used in making it e.g. white wine, fish stock, milk or light cream, and the type of flavourings e.g. fresh parsley, cheese, curry powder, finely

chopped button mushrooms, cooked chopped onion, cooked chopped prawns etc.

White Sauce

Serves 4

45g/3 tbsps butter
90g/6 tbsps white, plain flour
15fl oz/400ml whole milk
Salt and freshly ground black
    pepper

Melt the butter in a heavy saucepan, stir in the flour to form a roux and cook over a gentle heat, stirring, for 2 minutes.

Remove pan from heat and blend in a little of the milk, using a balloon whisk. Add the rest of the milk, gradually, whisking continually to ensure there are no lumps. Season.

Return to heat and bring to the boil, stirring all the time. Simmer gently for 5 minutes, stirring. Serve immediately.

Variations: To the above coating sauce one of the following may be added:-

Curry Sauce: Add 1 tsp curry powder, mixed with the flour.

Parsley Sauce: Add 1 tbsp freshly chopped parsley to the prepared sauce, just before serving.

Cheese Sauce: Add 3oz freshly grated, mature Cheddar cheese to the freshly-made sauce. Stir to melt, then serve immediately.

Mushroom Sauce: Add 2oz finely chopped button mushrooms to the prepared sauce. The mushrooms will cook in the intense heat of the sauce. Serve immediately.

Prawn Sauce: Add 3oz cooked,

shelled prawns to the completed sauce. Heat through gently over a low heat, stirring continuously, until very hot. Serve immediately.

Egg Sauce: Hard-boil, peel and finely chop 2 eggs and add to the sauce.

Onion Sauce: Add 1 medium onion, finely chopped and softened in a medium pan in 2 tbsps melted butter, to the completed sauce. Serve immediately.

Hollandaise Sauce

Serves 4

Serve this piquant sauce warm, rather than hot, with all types of fish. It is a particularly rich sauce and ideal on a special buffet table accompanying a whole, dressed salmon or a colourful mixed seafood platter.

45ml/3 tbsps tarragon vinegar
15ml/1 tbsp water
2 egg yolks
90g/6 tbsps butter
Salt and freshly ground black
    pepper

Put vinegar and water into a small non-stick pan and bring to the boil. Boil until reduced to about 1 tablespoon. Remove from heat and allow to cool slightly. Put the egg yolks into a bowl and stir in the vinegar. Set over a pan of hot water and heat gently, stirring all the time, until the egg mixture thickens. (Keep the water just gently simmering so that the egg does not overcook.) Divide butter into small pieces and gradually whisk into the sauce. Season to taste. The sauce should be the consistency of home-made

mayonnaise and golden yellow in colour. It should be slightly piquant in flavour.

Tartar Sauce

Serves 4

This popular sauce is traditionally served with fried fish and chips.

300ml/11fl oz fresh mayonnaise
    (see recipe)
2½ tsps chopped gherkins
2½ tsps chopped capers
125ml/5fl oz natural yogurt or
    single cream
1 tsp freshly chopped parsley or
    basil

Mix all ingredients together. Cover and refrigerate until ready to serve.

Gooseberry Sauce

Serves 4

This unusual sauce is pleasantly tart and therefore particularly good served with oily fish such as trout, mackerel and salmon. It may be made in advance and reheated just before serving. This sauce also freezes well.

15oz can gooseberries in natural
    juice
Grated rind ½ lemon
2½ tsps lemon juice
2½ tsps caster sugar
2 tbsps butter

Liquidize or process the gooseberries with their juice, until puréed. Turn into a medium saucepan. Add the lemon rind, juice, the sugar and the butter. Heat, over a medium heat, stirring constantly until simmering. Serve with fish of your choice.

Yogurt Sauce with Celery

Serves 4

A light, creamy sauce which is ideal to serve with fish kebabs, grilled salmon or whole, baked fish.

160ml/6fl oz natural yogurt
1 tsp concentrated mint sauce
1 tsp lemon juice
1 tsp clear honey
90ml/6 tbsps single cream
2 sticks celery, finely chopped

Mix all ingredients, except the celery, until well blended. Add celery and serve immediately.

Mayonnaise

Serves 4

Mayonnaise is simple to make using an electric blender or food processor. It can be varied in many ways according to taste and makes an excellent accompaniment to just about any fish dish.

1 tsp freshly-made English mustard
1 egg
1 egg yolk
45ml/3 tbsps lemon juice
280ml/10fl oz sunflower oil
Salt and freshly ground black pepper

Put the mustard, egg and egg yolk into the blender or food processor bowl. Blend or process for about 15 seconds. Leave the machine running and very slowly add the oil, a drop at a time at first, then slightly faster. Continue to process until the mayonnaise is thick and creamy. Add lemon juice and seasoning and process for a few seconds longer. Serve immediately or keep for up to 2 weeks in a screw-top jar in the refrigerator.

Variations

Curry Mayonnaise: Add 1 teaspoon curry powder or paste instead of the mustard.

Parsley Mayonnaise: Stir 1 tablespoon freshly chopped parsley into the prepared mayonnaise.

Tomato Mayonnaise: Add 1-2 tablespoons tomato purée to the mayonnaise when you add the lemon juice.

Garlic Mayonnaise: Add 3 cloves crushed garlic when you add the lemon juice.

Lemon and Basil Mayonnaise: Add grated rind of ½ lemon and 2 teaspoons finely chopped fresh basil when you add the lemon juice.

Bouillabaisse

Serves 4

60g/4 tbsps butter
1 stick celery, chopped
1 medium onion, chopped
1 clove garlic, crushed
1lb tomatoes, peeled and chopped
1lb white fish, such as cod
1 bouquet garni
Salt and freshly ground black pepper
80ml/3fl oz dry cider
1120ml/2 pints boiling water
1 x 7oz can tuna fish in brine, drained
100g/4oz cooked prawns
Freshly chopped parsley to garnish

Melt the butter in a large pan, then soften the celery, onion and garlic over a medium heat. Add the tomatoes and continue to cook, stirring occasionally for a further 5 minutes. Add the prepared white fish, cut into neat chunks with the bouquet garni, seasoning, and the cider. Pour on the boiling water. Cover with a lid, bring to the boil and boil fairly briskly for about 15 minutes. Add the flaked tuna and the shrimp and heat gently for 3 minutes. Remove bouquet garni, then using a draining spoon, lift fish and divide between soup dishes. Add liquid, then garnish with parsley and serve immediately.

Fish Chowder

Serves 4

1lb white fish fillets, washed
280ml/10fl oz milk
Salt and freshly ground black pepper
2 strips bacon, de-rinded and chopped
1 tbsp butter
225g/8oz potato, peeled and diced
2 medium carrots, diced
1 medium onion, chopped
430ml/15fl oz boiling chicken stock
3 tbsps cornstarch
Chopped parsley to garnish

Put fish into a saucepan with half the milk and simmer gently for 10 minutes. Drain fish, retaining milk and set aside, covered. Fry bacon in a clean, non-stick medium saucepan until crisp, add butter, then when melted, add onion and fry to soften. Add potato and carrot with reserved milk, remaining milk and the stock, simmer gently for 10-15 minutes, until potato and carrot are tender. Blend cornstarch with a little water and stir into the pan. Simmer for 5 minutes, stirring. Add fish with any juices, re-heat gently until thoroughly hot, and serve immediately, sprinkled with plenty of freshly chopped parsley.

Chapter I

Soups & Starters

SERVES 6-8

CREAMY SHELLFISH SOUP

Buy fresh or frozen cockles for this
filling recipe. The variety packed in brine
or vinegar will spoil the soup's taste.

90g/3oz rindless streaky bacon, diced
2 medium onions, finely diced
15ml/1 tbsp flour
6 medium potatoes, peeled and cubed
Salt and pepper
1150ml/2 pints milk
140ml/¼pint fish stock
280ml/½ pint single cream
450g/1lb fresh or frozen cockles
Chopped parsley (optional)

Step 2 Cook the onion in the bacon fat until soft and transluscent.

Step 3 Cook the onion in the bacon fat until soft and translucent.

Step 1 Cook the bacon slowly until the fat renders.

1. Place the diced bacon in a large, deep saucepan and cook slowly until the fat is rendered. Turn up the heat and brown the bacon. Remove it to paper towel to drain.

2. Add the onions to the bacon fat in the pan and cook slowly to soften. Stir in the flour and add the potatoes, salt, pepper, milk and fish stock.

3. Cover and bring to the boil and cook for about 10 minutes, or until the potatoes are nearly tender. Add cockles to the soup along with the cream and diced bacon. Cook a further 10 minutes, or until the potatoes and cockles are tender. Add the chopped parsley, if desired, and serve immediately.

Cook's Notes

 Time
Preparation takes about 30 minutes and cooking takes about 20 minutes.

 Cook's Tip
You can make your own fish stock or dissolve half of a fish stock cube in water.

 Buying Guide
Substitute either fresh, frozen or canned mussels, if preferred.

SERVES 4

HOT AND SOUR SEAFOOD SOUP

This interesting combination of flavours and ingredients
makes a sophisticated beginning to an informal meal.

3 dried Chinese mushrooms
1 tbsp vegetable oil
120g/4oz prawns, shelled and deveined
1 red chilli, seeded and finely sliced
1 green chilli, seeded and finely sliced
½ tsp lemon rind, cut into thin slivers
2 spring onions, sliced
560ml/1 pint fish stock
1 tbsp Worcestershire sauce
1 tbsp light soy sauce
60g/2oz whitefish fillets
1 cake of fresh bean curd, diced
1 tbsp lemon juice
1 tsp sesame seeds
Salt and pepper
1 tsp fresh coriander, finely chopped (optional)

3. Add the stock, the Worcestershire sauce and the soy sauce. Bring this mixture to the boil, reduce the heat and simmer for 5 minutes. Season to taste.

4. Remove the hard stalks from the mushrooms and discard them. Slice the caps very finely.

5. Cut the whitefish fillets into small dice, and add them to the soup, together with the bean curd and Chinese mushrooms. Simmer for a further 5 minutes.

6. Stir in the lemon juice and sesame seeds. Adjust the seasoning and serve sprinkled with chopped fresh coriander leaves, if desired.

Step 4 Remove the hard stalks from the reconstituted Chinese mushrooms and discard them. Slice the caps finely.

Step 1 Soak the dried Chinese mushrooms in boiling water for about 20 minutes, until they are completely reconstituted.

1. Soak the mushrooms in enough hot water to cover for 20 minutes, or until completely reconstituted.

2. Heat the vegetable oil in a large wok or frying pan, and add the prawns, chillies, lemon rind and spring onions. Stir-fry quickly for 1 minute.

Step 5 Cut the fish fillets into small dice, and add these to the soup mixture, together with the bean curd and shredded mushroom caps.

Cook's Notes

 Time
Preparation takes about 20 minutes, and cooking also takes about 20 minutes.

Cook's Tip
Dried Chinese mushrooms and fresh bean curd cakes can be bought in most delicatessens, or ethnic supermarkets.

Watchpoint
Care must be taken when using fresh chillies not to get the juice into the eyes or the mouth. If this should happen, rinse with lots of cold water.

SERVES 4

CREAMY CRAB SOUP

Serve this as an elegant starter
for special dinner parties.

1 large crab, cooked
45ml/3 tbsps butter or margarine
1 onion, very finely chopped
30g/2 tbsps flour
1150ml/2 pints milk
90ml/6 tbsps sherry
Pinch salt, white pepper and ground mace
140ml/¼ pint double cream, whipped
Red caviar or chopped chives

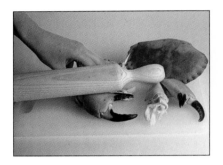

Step 1 Remove the legs and large claws of the crab. Use a rolling pin or meat mallet to crack the large claws and legs to extract the meat.

1. To dress the crab, take off all the legs and the large claws. Crack the large claws and legs and extract the meat.

2. Turn the crab shell over and press up with thumbs to push out the underbody. Cut this piece in quarters and use a skewer to pick out the meat. Discard the stomach sac and the lungs (dead man's fingers). Set the white meat aside with the claw meat.

Step 2 Turn the crab shell over and push out the underbody. Discard stomach sac and lungs.

3. Using a teaspoon, scrape out the brown meat from inside the shell and reserve it. If the roe is present reserve that, too.

4. Melt the butter or margarine in a medium saucepan and soften the onion for about 3 minutes. Do not allow to brown.

5. Stir in the flour and milk. Bring to the boil and then immediately turn down the heat to simmer. Add the brown meat from the crab and cook gently for about 20 minutes.

Step 3 Using a teaspoon, scrape out the brown meat from inside the shell.

6. Add the sherry, salt, pepper, mace, white crab meat and roe. Cook a further 5 minutes.

7. Top each serving with a spoonful of whipped cream and red caviar or chopped chives.

Cook's Notes

Time
Preparation takes about 35-40 minutes and cooking takes about 25 minutes.

Variation
Frozen crab meat may be substituted. Use about 4-6oz of white crab meat and omit the addition of the brown body meat. Do not use a dressed crab as the brown meat will often have breadcrumbs added to it.

Buying Guide
Buy a crab that is heavy for its size.

SERVES 6
PRAWN SOUP

A hearty soup that makes a meal
accompanied by some crusty bread.

45g/3 tbsps butter or margarine
1 onion, finely chopped
1 red pepper, seeded and finely chopped
2 sticks celery, finely chopped
1 clove garlic, minced
Pinch dry mustard
10ml/2 tsps paprika
45g/3 tbsps flour
1150ml/2 pints fish stock
1 sprig thyme and bay leaf
225g/8oz raw, peeled prawns
Salt and pepper
Snipped chives

3. Pour on the stock gradually, stirring until well blended. Add the thyme and bay leaf and bring to the boil. Reduce the heat and simmer about 5 minutes or until thickened, stirring occasionally.

4. Add the prawns and cook until pink and curled, about 5 minutes. Season with salt and pepper to taste and top with snipped chives before serving.

Step 3 Pour on the stock gradually and stir or whisk until well blended.

Step 2 Cook the mustard, cayenne, paprika and flour briefly until the mixture darkens in colour.

Step 4 Use kitchen scissors to snip the chives finely over the top of the soup before serving.

1. Melt the butter or margarine and add the onion, pepper, celery and garlic. Cook gently to soften.

2. Stir in the mustard, paprika and flour. Cook about 3 minutes over gentle heat, stirring occasionally.

Cook's Notes

Time
Preparation takes about 20 minutes and cooking takes about 8-10 minutes.

Variation
If using peeled, cooked prawns add just before serving and heat through for about 2 minutes only.

Cook's Tip
Cook spices such as paprika briefly before adding any liquid to develop their flavour and eliminate harsh taste.

SERVES 4

TOMATO FISH STEW

Cook any white fish you like
in this tomato sauce. Serve
with rice or potatoes.

Fishbones
1 bay leaf, 1 sprig thyme and 2 parsley stalks
2 slices onion
1 lemon slice
6 black peppercorns
430ml/¾ pint water
90ml/6 tbsps oil
90g/6 tbsps flour
1 large green pepper, seeded and finely chopped
1 onion, finely chopped
1 stick celery, finely chopped
900g/2lbs canned tomatoes
30g/2 tbsps tomato purée
Pinch salt and allspice
90ml/6 tbsps white wine
2 whole plaice, filleted and skinned
30ml/2 tbsps chopped parsley

3. Add the green pepper, onion and celery, and cook until the flour is a rich dark brown and the vegetables have softened.

4. Add stock and the canned tomatoes, tomato purée, salt and allspice. Bring to the boil and then simmer until thick. Add the wine.

5. Cut the fish fillets into 5cm/2 inch pieces and add to the tomato mixture. Cook slowly for about 20 minutes, or until the fish is tender. Gently stir in the parsley, taking care that the fish does not break up. Adjust the seasoning and serve.

Step 4 Simmer the tomato mixture until very thick.

Step 4 Pour the fish stock onto the oil and flour mixture, whisking constantly to form a smooth paste.

1. Place fish bones, herbs, onion, lemon slice, peppercorns and water in a saucepan. Bring to the boil, then simmer 20 minutes and strain.

2. Heat the oil and add the flour. Cook slowly, stirring constantly, until golden brown

Step 5 Cut the fish fillets into 5cm/2 inch pieces and add to the tomato mixture.

Cook's Notes

Time
Preparation takes about 30 minutes and cooking takes about 20 minutes for the fish stock and 20 minutes to finish the dish.

Preparation
Fish stock can be prepared a day in advance and refrigerated. It can also be frozen.

Variation
Wine may be replaced with 45ml/3 tbsps lemon juice and 45ml/5 tbsps water.

SERVES 4-6

CRAB AND SWEETCORN SOUP

Creamy sweetcorn and succulent crabmeat
combine to make a velvety rich soup. Whisked
egg whites add an interesting texture.

1 litre/1¾ pints chicken or fish stock
340g/12oz creamed sweetcorn
120g/4oz crabmeat
Salt and pepper
5ml/1 tsp light soy sauce
30ml/2 tbsps cornflour
45ml/3 tbsps water or stock
4 spring onions for garnish
2 egg whites, whisked
4 spring onions for garnish

Step 3 Whisk the egg whites until soft peaks form and stir into the hot soup.

Step 2 Mix the cornflour and water together with some of the hot soup and return the mixture to the pan.

1. Bring the stock to the boil in a large pan. Add the sweetcorn, crabmeat, seasoning and soy sauce. Allow to simmer for 4-5 minutes.

2. Mix the cornflour and water or stock and add a spoonful of the hot soup. Return the mixture to the soup and bring back to the boil. Cook until the soup thickens.

3. Whisk the egg whites until soft peaks form. Stir into the hot soup just before serving.

4. Slice the onions thinly on the diagonal and scatter over the top to serve.

Cook's Notes

Time
Preparation takes about 10 minutes, cooking takes about 8-10 minutes.

Preparation
Adding the egg whites is optional.

Watchpoint
Do not allow the sweetcorn and the crab to boil rapidly; they will both toughen.

Economy
Use crab sticks instead of crabmeat.

Variation
Chicken may be used instead of the crabmeat and the cooking time increased to 10-12 minutes.

SERVES 4

BOUILLABAISSE

This extra special soup is perfect for
impressing those special guests.

Stock
450g/1lb fish bones, skin and heads
1700ml/3 pints water
1 small onion, thinly sliced
1 small carrot, thinly sliced
1 bay leaf
6 black peppercorns
1 blade mace
1 sprig thyme
1 lemon slices

Bouillabaisse
45g/2½oz butter or margarine
1 carrot, sliced
3 leeks, well washed and thinly sliced
1 clove garlic
Pinch saffron
80ml–125ml dry white wine
225g/8oz canned tomatoes
1 lobster
450g/1lb cod or halibut fillets
450g/1lb mussels, well scrubbed
450g/1lb small clams, well scrubbed
8 new potatoes, scrubbed but not peeled
Chopped parsley
225g/8oz large prawns, peeled and de-veined

1. First prepare the fish stock. Place all the stock ingredients in a large stock pot and bring to the boil over high heat. Lower the heat and allow to simmer for 20 minutes. Strain and reserve the stock. Discard the fish bones and vegetables.

2. Melt the butter in a medium-sized saucepan and add the carrots, leeks and garlic. Cook for about 5 minutes until slightly softened.

3. Add the saffron and wine and allow to simmer for about 5 minutes.

4. Add the fish stock along with all the remaining bouillabaisse ingredients except the prawns. Bring the mixture to the boil and cook until the lobster turns red, the mussel and clam shells open and the potatoes are tender. Turn off the heat and add the prawns. Cover the pan and let the prawns cook in the residual heat. Divide the ingredients among 4 soup bowls. Remove the lobster and cut it in half. Divide the tail between the other 2 bowls and serve the bouillabaisse with garlic bread.

Step 2 Cook the carrots, leeks and garlic in butter until soft but not coloured. Combine all the bouillabaisse ingredients in a large stock pot.

Step 4 Remove the lobster and cut it in half using a large, sharp knife.

Cook's Notes

Time
Preparation takes about 35 minutes and cooking takes about 30 minutes.

Watchpoint
Leeks must be split in half first and rinsed under cold water to remove sand and grit before slicing.

Variation
Use whatever shellfish or fish is in season or suits your taste. Lobster is not essential.

SERVES 4
MUSSELS IN WHITE WINE SAUCE

Mussels in season are very economical.
Most fishmongers sell them and so do
supermarkets that have fresh fish counters.

2kg/4½lbs mussels in their shells
Flour or cornmeal
280ml/½ pint dry white wine
1 large onion, finely chopped
2-4 cloves garlic, finely chopped
Salt and coarsely ground black pepper
2 bay leaves
225g/8oz butter, melted
Juice of 1 lemon

1. Scrub the mussels well and remove any barnacles and beards (seaweed strands). Use a stiff brush to scrub the shells, and discard any mussels with broken shells or those that do not close when tapped.

2. Place the mussels in a basin full of cold water with a handful of flour and leave to soak for 30 minutes.

3. Drain the mussels and place them in a large, deep saucepan with the remaining ingredients, except the butter and lemon juice. Cover the pan and bring to the boil.

4. Stir the mussels occasionally while they are cooking to help them cook evenly. Cook about 5-8 minutes, or until the shells open. Discard any mussels that do not open.

5. Spoon the mussels into individual serving bowls and strain the cooking liquid. Pour the liquid into 4 small bowls and serve with the mussels and a bowl of melted butter mixed with lemon juice for each person. Dip the mussels into the broth and the melted butter to eat. Use a mussel shell to scoop out each mussel, or eat with small forks or spoons.

Step 1 Scrub the mussels with a stiff brush to remove barnacles and seaweed beards.

Step 1 To test if the mussels are still alive, tap them on a work surface – the shells should close.

Step 5 Hold a mussel shell between 2 fingers and pinch together to remove mussels from their shells to eat.

Cook's Notes

Time
Preparation takes about 30 minutes, and cooking takes about 5-8 minutes.

Cook's Tip
The beards are strands of seaweed that anchor the mussels to the rocks on which they grow. These must be removed before cooking. They can be pulled off quite easily by hand, or scrubbed off with a stiff brush.

Variation
Use the amount of garlic that suits your own taste or leave out the garlic, if desired. Chopped fresh herbs may be added.

SERVES 6

PRAWN AND CHICKEN PEPPERS

Try a stuffing that is different from the usual meat
and rice one for lighter tasting peppers.

3 large green or red peppers
60g/4 tbsps butter or margarine
1 small onion, finely chopped
1 stick celery, finely chopped
1 clove garlic, crushed
2 chicken breasts, skinned, boned and diced
175g/5oz cooked, peeled prawns
10ml/2 tsps chopped parsley
½ loaf of stale bread, made into crumbs
1-2 eggs, beaten
Salt and pepper
90g/6 tsps dry breadcrumbs

Step 1 Cut peppers in half and remove seeds and white core.

1. Cut the pepper in half lengthwise and remove the cores and seeds. Leave the stems attached, if desired.

2. Melt the butter in a large frying pan and add the onion, celery, garlic and chicken. Cook over moderate heat until the vegetables are softened and the chicken is cooked. Add the prawns and parsley. Season with salt and pepper.

3. Stir in the stale breadcrumbs and add enough beaten egg to make the mixture hold together.

Step 4 Spoon filling into the pepper halves, mounding the top and smoothing out.

4. Spoon filling into each pepper half, mounding the top slightly. Place the peppers in a baking dish that holds them closely.

5. Pour enough water down the side of the dish to come about 1.25cm/½ inch up the sides of the peppers. Cover and bake in a pre-heated 180°C/350°F/Gas Mark 4 oven for about 45 minutes, or until the peppers are just tender.

Step 5 Place peppers close together in a baking dish and carefully pour in about 1.25cm/½ inch water.

6. Sprinkle each with the dried breadcrumbs and place under a preheated grill until golden brown.

Cook's Notes

Time
Preparation takes about 30 minutes and cooking takes about 45-50 minutes.

Variations
Use spring onions in place of the small onion. Add chopped nuts or black olives to the filling, if desired.

Serving Ideas
Serve as a first course, either hot or cold, or as a light lunch or supper with a salad.

SERVES 2-4

SPICY BAKED PRAWNS

This recipe is popular everywhere
succulent prawns are available.

2 dozen raw large prawns, unpeeled
60g/4 tbsps butter or margarine
1 small red pepper, seeded and finely chopped
2 spring onions, finely chopped
½ tsp dry mustard
10ml/2 tsps dry sherry
1 tsp Worcester sauce
100g/4oz cooked crab meat
6 tbsps fresh breadcrumbs
1 tbsp chopped parsley
30ml/2 tbsps mayonnaise
Salt and pepper
1 small egg, beaten
Grated Parmesan cheese
Paprika

1. Remove all of the prawn shells except for the very tail ends.

2. Remove the black veins on the rounded sides.

3. Cut the prawn down the length of the curved side and press each one open.

4. Melt half of the butter or margarine in a small pan and cook the pepper to soften, about 3 minutes. Add the spring onions and cook a further 2 minutes.

5. Combine the peppers with the mustard, sherry, Worcester sauce, crab meat, breadcrumbs, parsley and mayonnaise. Add seasoning and enough egg to bind together.

6. Spoon the stuffing onto the prawns and sprinkle with the Parmesan cheese and paprika. Melt the remaining butter or margarine and drizzle over the prawns.

7. Bake in a pre-heated 180°C/350°F/Gas Mark 4 oven for about 10 minutes. Serve immediately.

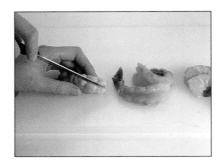

Step 3 Cut the prawn down the length of the curved side and press each one open.

Step 6 Spoon the stuffing onto the prawn, pressing down lightly to spread prawn open.

Cook's Notes

 Time
Preparation takes about 30 minutes and cooking takes about 15 minutes.

 Variation
Try chopped black or green olives in the stuffing for a change of flavour. Mushrooms may be cooked with the red pepper and spring onions, if desired, and other herbs substituted for parsley.

 Serving Ideas
Serve as a starter or as a main course for 2 people.

SERVES 4

OREGANO OYSTERS

The combination of oregano and the anise taste
of Pernod is an unusual but very complementary
one, especially with fresh oysters.

1 tbsp butter or margarine
1 clove garlic, crushed
1 tbsp chopped parsley
1 tbsp chopped fresh oregano or 1½ tsps dried
   oregano
1 tbsp Pernod
180g/6fl oz double cream
Salt and pepper
24 oysters on the half shell
12 strips bacon, cooked and crumbled
Course salt

1. Melt the butter or margarine in a saucepan. Add the garlic and cook to soften, but do not brown.

2. Add the parsley, oregano, Pernod and cream. Bring to the boil and lower the heat to simmering. Strain on any liquid from the oysters and then loosen them from their shells with a small, sharp knife.

3. Cook the mixture until reduced by about one quarter and slightly thickened. Test the seasoning and set the mixture aside.

4. Pour about 1 inch coarse salt into a baking pan.

5. Place the oysters on top of the salt and twist the shells into the salt so that they stand level.

6. Spoon some of the cream over each oyster and sprinkle with the crumbled bacon.

7. Bake in a pre-heated 200°C/400°F/Gas Mark 6 oven for 15-18 minutes. Serve immediately.

Step 2 Using a small, sharp knife loosen the oyster from its shell.

Step 3 Cook mixture until reduced by a quarter.

Step 5 Place the oysters in their shells into the course salt, twisting so that they stand level.

Cook's Notes

Time
Preparation takes about 25 minutes. Cooking takes about 20-25 minutes including time to cook the bacon.

Buying Guide
It is possible to purchase oysters already on the half shell. If you need to open them yourself, buy a special oyster knife with a short, strong blade. Insert the blade at the hinge and twist until shells separate.

Variation
If oysters are unavailable use mussels or clams.

SERVES 6-8

CRAB MEAT BALLS

Delicious as a first course or a cocktail
snack, crab meat balls can be made ahead,
then coated and fried at the last minute.

1lb fresh or frozen crab meat, chopped finely
4 slices white bread, crusts removed and made into
   crumbs
1 tbsp butter or margarine
1 tbsp flour
120ml/4fl oz milk
½ red or green chilli, seeded and finely chopped
1 spring onion, finely chopped
1 tbsp chopped parsley
Salt
Flour
2 eggs, beaten
Dry breadcrumbs
Oil for frying

Step 4 Flour hands well and shape cold crab mixture into balls.

Step 5 Brush on beaten egg or dip into egg to coat.

1. Combine the crab meat with the fresh breadcrumbs and set aside.

2. Melt the butter and add the flour off the heat. Stir in the milk and return to moderate heat. Bring to the boil, stirring constantly.

3. Stir the white sauce into the crab meat and breadcrumbs, adding the chilli, onion and parsley. Season with salt to taste, cover and allow to cool completely.

4. Shape the cold mixture into 1 inch balls with floured hands.

5. Coat with beaten egg using a fork to turn balls in the mixture or use a pastry brush to coat with egg.

6. Coat with the dry breadcrumbs.

7. Fry in oil in a deep sauté pan, saucepan or deep-fat fryer at 180°C/350°F until golden brown and crisp, about 3 minutes per batch of 6. Turn occasionally while frying.

8. Drain on paper and sprinkle lightly with salt.

Cook's Notes

Time
Preparation takes about 40-50 minutes, including time for the mixture to cool. A batch of 6 balls takes about 3 minutes to cook.

Variation
Use finely chopped prawns instead of crab meat. Omit chilli if desired, or use a quarter red or green pepper.

£ Economy
Cooked whitefish such as haddock or whiting can be substituted for half of the crab meat. Crab sticks can also be used.

SERVES 4

OYSTERS ROCKEFELLER

Oysters can be purchased already opened,
and you'll find the rest of this famous American
dish simplicity itself to prepare.

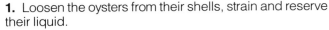

24 oysters on the half shell
Rock salt
6 strips bacon, finely chopped
560g/1¼lbs fresh spinach, well washed, stems
    removed and leaves finely chopped
1 small bunch spring onions, finely chopped
2 cloves garlic, crushed
4-5 tbsps fine fresh breadcrumbs
Dash Tabasco
30ml/2 tbsps aniseed liqueur
Pinch salt
Parmesan cheese

1. Loosen the oysters from their shells, strain and reserve their liquid.

2. Rinse the shells well and return an oyster to each one. Pour about 1 inch of rock salt into a baking pan and place in the oysters in their shells, pressing each shell gently into the salt.

3. Place the bacon in a large frying pan and cook slowly to render the fat. Turn up the heat and brown the bacon evenly.

4. Add the spinach, spring onions and garlic and cook slowly until softened. Add the breadcrumbs, Tabasco, oyster liquid, liqueur, and a pinch of salt.

5. Spoon some of the mixture onto each oyster and sprinkle with Parmesan cheese. Place in a preheated 180°C/350°F/Gas Mark 4 oven for about 15 minutes. Alternatively, heat through in the oven for 10 minutes and place under a preheated grill to lightly brown the cheese. Serve immediately.

Step 1 With a small sharp knife loosen the oysters from their shells to make them easier to eat. Hold over bowl to catch liquid.

Step 2 Press the oyster shells into a baking pan filled with salt so that the shells sit level.

Step 5 Spoon in the prepared mixture to cover each oyster completely.

Cook's Notes

Time
Preparation takes about 25 minutes or longer if opening the oysters yourself. Cooking takes about 25 minutes.

£ Buying Guide
It is possible to purchase oysters already on the half shell. If you need to open them yourself, buy a special oyster knife with a short, strong blade.

Variation
Finely chopped anchovies may be used instead of the bacon, and 3 tbsps butter or margarine substituted for the bacon fat.

SERVES 2-4

CREAMY DRESSED CRAB

This makes a delicious warm weather salad for
lunches, light suppers or elegant starters.

2 small crabs, boiled
30ml/2 tbsps oil
4 spring onions
1 small green pepper, seeded and finely chopped
1 stick celery, finely chopped
1 clove garlic, crushed
180ml/6 fl oz prepared mayonnaise
15ml/1 tbsp mild mustard
Dash tabasco and Worcestershire sauce
1 piece canned pimento, drained and finely chopped
30ml/2 tbsps chopped parsley
Salt and pepper
Lettuce

1. To shell the crabs, first remove all the legs and the large claws by twisting and pulling them away from the body.

2. Turn the shell over and, using your thumbs, push the body away from the flat shell. Set the body aside.

3. Remove the stomach sack and the lungs or dead man's fingers and discard them. Using a small teaspoon, scrape the brown body meat out of the flat shell.

4. Using a sharp knife, cut the body of the crab in four pieces and using a pick or a skewer, push out all the meat.

5. Crack the large claws and remove the meat in one piece if possible. Crack the legs and remove the meat as well, leaving the small, thin legs in the shell. Set all the meat aside. Scrub the shells if desired to use for serving.

6. Heat the oil in a small sauté pan or frying pan. Chop the white parts of the spring onions and add to the oil with the green pepper, celery and garlic. Sauté over gentle heat for about 10 minutes, stirring often to soften the vegetables but not brown them. Remove from the heat and set aside. When cool, add the mayonnaise, mustard, tabasco, Worcestershire sauce, pimento and finely chopped tops of the spring onions.

7. Spoon the reserved brown body meat from the crabs back into each shell or serving dish. Mix the remaining crab meat with the dressing, reserving the crab claws for garnish, if desired. They may also be shredded and added to the other crab meat. Do not overmix the sauce as the crab meat should stay in large pieces. Spoon into the shells on top of the brown body meat, sprinkle with chopped parsley and place the crab shells on serving plates, surrounding them with lettuce leaves, if desired. Garnish with the shelled crab claws and use the crab legs if desired. Sprinkle with parsley and serve immediately.

Step 3 Discard the plastic-like stomach sack and spongy lungs. Remove brown body meat from the shell of the crab and reserve it.

Step 4 Cut through the body of the crab with a sharp knife and pick out the crab meat with a skewer.

Cook's Notes

Time
Preparation takes about 45 minutes, cooking takes about 10 minutes.

Variation
If desired, recipe can be prepared with dressed or frozen crab meat. Allow about 90-120g/3-4 oz crab meat per person.

£ Buying Guide
Precooked crabs may be purchased from fishmongers or fish markets. Use on the day of purchase.

SERVES 4

PRAWNS ACAPULCO

These make a stylish starter or a quickly
prepared snack. Make the bread slices
smaller to serve with cocktails.

4 slices bread, crusts removed
90g/6 tbsps softened butter
180g/6oz cooked and peeled prawns
2.5ml/½ tsp chilli powder
1.25ml/¼ tsp paprika
1.25ml/¼ tsp cumin
Salt and pepper
Watercress to garnish

1. Cut the bread slices in half and spread with 30g/2 tbsps butter. Butter both sides sparingly.

2. Place the bread on a baking sheet and cook in a preheated 180°C/350°F/Gas Mark 4 oven for 10-15 minutes until golden brown. Keep warm.

3. Melt the remaining butter in a small pan and add the prawns, spices and seasoning and stir well.

4. Heat through completely and spoon on top of the bread slices. Garnish with watercress and serve hot.

Step 2 Cook the bread on a baking sheet until golden brown and crisp.

Step 3 Cook the prawn and chilli mixture over gentle heat, stirring continuously.

Cook's Notes

Time
Preparation takes about 15 minutes. The bread will take 15-20 minutes to cook until golden, and the prawns take about 5 minutes to heat through.

Watchpoint
Do not heat the prawns too long or at too high a temperature; they toughen easily.

Cook's Tip
The bread may be prepared in advance and reheated 5 minutes in the oven. Do not reheat the prawns.

SERVES 4-6

QUICK FRIED PRAWNS

Prepared with either raw or cooked
prawns, this is an incredibly delicious
starter that is extremely easy to cook.

900g/2lbs cooked prawns in their shells
2 cloves garlic, crushed
2.5cm/1 inch piece fresh ginger, finely chopped
15ml/1 tbsp chopped fresh Chinese parsley (coriander)
45ml/3 tbsps oil
15ml/1 tbsp rice wine or dry sherry
25ml/1½ tbsps light soy sauce
Chopped spring onions to garnish

Step 2 Peel the
shells from the
prawns, leaving
only the tail ends
on.

Step 1 Carefully
pull the head of
the prawn away
from the body.

1. Shell the prawns except for the very tail ends. Place the
prawns in a bowl with the remaining ingredients, except for
the garnish, and leave to marinate for 30 minutes.

2. Heat the wok and add the prawns and their marinade.
Stir-fry briefly to heat the prawns.

3. Chop the onions roughly or cut into neat rounds.
Sprinkle over the prawns to serve.

Cook's Notes

Time
Preparation takes about 30
minutes for the prawns to
marinate. Cooking takes about 2
minutes.

Watchpoint
Do not overcook the prawns
as they will toughen.

Variation
If uncooked prawns are
available, stir-fry with their
marinade until they turn pink.

SERVES 4

MUSSELS IN RED WINE

Red wine makes an unusual, but very pleasant,
combination with seafood. This recipe is equally
good with clams or cockles.

1.5kg/3lb mussels, well scrubbed
280ml/½ pint dry red wine
90ml/6 tbsps olive oil
4 cloves garlic, finely chopped
2 bay leaves
30ml/2 tbsps fresh thyme, chopped
90ml/6 tbsps red wine vinegar
5ml/1 tsp paprika
Grated rind and juice of 1 lemon
Salt and pepper
Pinch cayenne pepper
Pinch sugar (optional)
Chopped parsley

Step 1
Cook the mussels over high heat, stirring frequently, until the shells begin to open.

1. Prepare the mussels as in the recipe for Paella. Place the wine in a large saucepan and bring to the boil. Add the mussels, cover the pan and cook briskly for about 4-5 minutes, stirring frequently, until the shells open. Discard any that do not open.

2. Transfer the mussels to a bowl and pour the cooking liquid through a fine strainer and reserve it.

Step 2
Transfer the mussels to a plate and pour the liquid through a fine strainer or through muslin.

3. In a clean saucepan, heat the oil and fry the garlic over gentle heat until golden brown. Add the bay leaves, thyme, vinegar, paprika, lemon juice and rind, salt, pepper and cayenne pepper. Pour on the wine, add sugar, if using, and bring to the boil. Cook to reduce to about 180ml/6 fl oz. Allow to cool completely.

4. Remove the mussels from their shells and add them to the liquid, stirring to coat all the mussels. Cover and place in the refrigerator for at least 2 hours. Allow to stand at room temperature for about 30 minutes before serving. Sprinkle with parsley.

Step 4
Remove the mussels from their shells with your fingers or by using a small teaspoon.

Cook's Notes

Time
Preparation takes about 30 minutes and cooking takes about 9-10 minutes.

Serving Ideas
Serve in small dishes as tapas. To serve as a more formal first course, place lettuce leaves on individual plates and spoon on the mussels. Sprinkle with chopped parsley, if desired.

Variation
Shelled mussels, purchased from a fishmonger, or frozen mussels may be used instead. If using frozen mussels, allow a further 2-3 minutes cooking time.

SERVES 4

FRIED FISH WITH GARLIC SAUCE

Fish in such an attractive shape makes an
excellent first course.

900g/2lbs fresh anchovies or whitebait
120g/4oz plain flour
60-90ml/4-6 tbsps cold water
Pinch salt
Oil for frying

Garlic Sauce

4 slices bread, crusts trimmed, soaked in water for 10
    minutes
4 cloves garlic, peeled and roughly chopped
30ml/2 tbsps lemon juice
60-75ml/4-5 tbsps olive oil
15-30ml/1-2 tbsps water (optional)
Salt and pepper
10ml/2 tsps chopped fresh parsley
Lemon wedges for garnishing (optional)

1. Sift the flour into a deep bowl with a pinch of salt.
Gradually stir in the water in the amount needed to make a
very thick batter.

2. Heat enough oil for frying in a large, deep pan. A deep-
sided sauté pan is ideal.

3. Take 3 fish at a time and dip them into the batter together.
Press their tails together firmly to make a fan shape.

4. Lower them carefully into the oil. Fry in several batches
until crisp and golden. Continue in the same way with all the
remaining fish.

Step 3 Dip three
fish at a time into
the batter and
when coated
press the tails
together firmly to
form a fan shape.

Step 4 Lower the
fish carefully into
the hot oil to
preserve the
shape.

5. Meanwhile, squeeze out the bread and place in a food
processor with the garlic and lemon juice. With the processor running, add the oil in a thin, steady stream. Add
water if the mixture is too thick and dry. Add salt and pepper
and stir in the parsley by hand. When all the fish are cooked,
sprinkle lightly with salt and arrange on serving plates with
some of the garlic sauce and lemon wedges, if desired.

Cook's Notes

Time
Preparation takes about 30
minutes, cooking takes about
3 minutes per batch for the fish.

Preparation
Coat the fish in the batter just
before ready for frying.

Cook's Tip
The fish should be eaten
immediately after frying. If it is
necessary to keep the fish warm, place
them on a wire cooling rack covered
with paper towels in a slow oven with
the door open. Sprinkling fried food
lightly with salt helps to absorb excess
fat.

Variation
Fish may be dipped in the
batter and fried singly if
desired. Other fish, such as smelt or
sardines, may also be used. Use thin
strips of cod or halibut as well. Vary the
amount of garlic in the sauce to your
own taste.

SERVES 4

FRIED SQUID

Serve this sweet and delicious seafood
as a starter or main course. It's
easier to prepare than you think!

675g/1½lb fresh squid
60g/2oz plain flour
Salt and pepper
Oil for deep-frying
Lemon wedges and parsley for garnishing

Step 2 Cut the tentacles from the head just below the eye and separate them into individual pieces.

1. Hold the body of the squid with one hand and the head with the other and pull gently to separate. Remove the intestines and the quill, which is clear and plastic-like. Rinse the body of the squid inside and outside under cold running water.

2. Cut the tentacles from the head, just above the eye. Separate into individual tentacles.

3. Remove the brownish or purplish outer skin from the body of the squid and cut the flesh into 5mm/¼ inch rings.

4. Mix the flour, salt and pepper together on a sheet of paper or in a shallow dish. Toss the rings of squid and the tentacles in the flour mixture to coat. Heat the oil to 180°C/350°F and fry the squid, about 6 pieces at a time, saving the tentacles until last. Remove them from the oil when brown and crisp with a draining spoon and place on

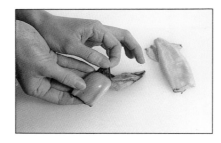

Step 3 Remove the outer skin from the body of the squid and cut the body into thin rings.

paper towels. Sprinkle lightly with salt and continue with the remaining squid. The pieces will take about 3 minutes to cook. Place on serving dishes and garnish each dish with a wedge of lemon and some parsley.

Cook's Notes

Time
Preparation takes about 25 minutes, cooking takes 3 minutes per batch of 6 pieces.

Serving Ideas
Sprinkle the squid with chopped fresh oregano just before serving.

Preparation
Do not coat the pieces of squid too soon before frying or they will become soggy.

Watchpoint
Once the squid is added to the hot oil, cover the fryer as the oil will tend to spatter.

Cook's Tip
If the squid must be re-heated, spread the pieces on wire cooling racks covered with paper towels and place in a slow oven for about 10 minutes. Do not re-fry, as this toughens the squid.

SERVES 4-6

PRAWNS MARINATED IN WHITE WINE

Dishes like this one from Schleswig-Holstein have a distinctly Scandinavian flavour, despite the use of an unmistakably German wine.

900g/2lbs peeled uncooked prawns

Marinade

280ml/½ pint Mosel wine
60ml/4 tbsps lemon juice
15ml/1 tbsp chopped fresh dill
Pinch salt and black pepper
1 clove garlic, crushed
1 bay leaf
Chopped parsley for garnishing
60ml/4 tbsps butter or margarine

Step 1 Peel the shrimp and remove any black veins along the rounded side.

1. Peel the prawns and remove the black vein along the top. If desired, the tail ends of the shell may be left attached. Place the prawns in a shallow dish.

2. Combine all the marinade ingredients except the chopped parsley and the butter. Pour the marinade over the prawns and turn several times to coat well. Marinate for at least 2 hours in the refrigerator.

3. Melt the butter or margarine in a large frying pan. Remove the prawns from the marinade with a slotted spoon and place them in the butter. Cook over moderate heat for 8-10 minutes, stirring frequently for even cooking.

4. Pour the marinade into a deep saucepan. Boil rapidly until it thickens and reduces by about ¾.

5. Place the cooked prawns in a large serving dish or in individual dishes and pour over the reduced marinade. Sprinkle with chopped parsley and serve immediately.

Step 3 When the prawns are cooked, they will curl up slightly, become opaque and turn pink. Do not over cook them or they will toughen.

Step 4 Place the marinade in a saucepan and boil rapidly to reduce to a syrupy consistency.

Cook's Notes

Watchpoint
Do not cook the prawns too long or over heat that is too high as they will toughen.

Cook's Tip
If serving cold, the prawns may be prepared a day in advance.

Serving Ideas
Serve the prawns with rolls or brown bread. If serving cold, chill well and serve on a bed of lettuce leaves.

SERVES 4-6

SWORDFISH KEBABS

Swordfish is one of the most commonly caught fish
in Southern Italy and Sicily. It won't fall apart
during cooking − a bonus when making kebabs.

1kg/2¼lbs swordfish steaks
90ml/6 tbsps olive oil
5ml/1 tsp chopped oregano
5ml/1 tsp chopped marjoram
Juice and rind of ½ a lemon
4 tomatoes, cut in thick slices
2 lemons, cut in thin slices
Salt and freshly ground pepper
Lemon slices and Italian parsley for garnish

1. Cut the swordfish steaks into 5cm/2 inch pieces.

2. Mix the olive oil, herbs, lemon juice and rind together and set it aside. Thread the swordfish, tomato slices and lemon slices on skewers, alternating the ingredients. Brush the skewers with the oil and lemon juice mixture and cook under a preheated grill for about 10 minutes, basting frequently with the lemon and oil. Serve garnished with lemons and parsley.

Step 1 Cut the swordfish steaks into even-sized pieces.

Step 2 Thread the ingredients onto the skewers, alternating the colours.

Cook's Notes

Time
Preparation takes about 15 minutes, cooking takes about 10 minutes.

Variations
Fresh tuna may be used instead of swordfish. Use cherry tomatoes instead of sliced tomatoes, if available.

Serving Ideas
Accompany the kebabs with risotto and a green salad.

SERVES 4

MOULES MARINIÈRE

Brittany and Normandy are famous for mussels and for cream and so cooks combined the two in one perfect seafood dish.

1.5kg/3lbs mussels
430ml/¾ pint dry cider or white wine
4 shallots, finely chopped
1 clove garlic, crushed
1 bouquet garni
140ml/¼ pint double cream
45g/3 tbsps butter, cut into small pieces
30ml/2 tbsps finely chopped parsley

1. Scrub the mussels well and remove the beards and any barnacles from the shells. Discard any mussels that have cracked shells and do not open when lightly tapped. Put the mussels into a large bowl and soak in cold water for at least 1 hour. Meanwhile, chop the parsley very finely.

2. Bring the cider or wine to the boil in a large stock pot and add the shallots, garlic and bouquet garni. Add the mussels, cover the pan and cook for 5 minutes. Shake the pan or stir the mussels around frequently until the shells open. Lift out the mussels into a large soup tureen or individual serving bowls. Discard any mussels that have not opened.

3. Reduce the cooking liquid by about half and strain into another saucepan. Add the cream and bring to the boil to thicken slightly. Beat in the butter, a few pieces at a time. Adjust the seasoning, add the parsley and pour the sauce over the mussels to serve.

Step 1 Break off thick stems from parsley and chop leaves very finely.

Step 2 Whilst cooking the mussels, stir or shake them frequently until the shells open.

Step 3 Beat the butter into the thickened cream and cooking liquid, a few pieces at a time.

Cook's Notes

Preparation
Soak mussels with a handful of flour or cornmeal in the water. They will then expel sand and take up the flour or cornmeal, which plumps them up.

Serving Ideas
Serve as a first course with French bread, or double the quantity of mussels to serve for a light main course.

Time
Preparation takes about 30 minutes, cooking takes about 15 minutes.

SERVES 6
FISH ESCABECH

Originally, this method of marinating sautéed fish in vinegar was simply a way of preserving it. All kinds of fish and even poultry and game were prepared this way.

900g/3lb monkfish
90g/6 tbsps flour
Pinch salt and pepper
1 medium carrot, peeled and thinly sliced
1 medium onion, thinly sliced
1 bay leaf
2 sprigs parsley
¼-½ fresh red chilli, finely chopped
340ml/12 fl oz white wine vinegar
6 cloves garlic, peeled and thinly sliced
Olive oil

1. Peel the brownish membrane from the outside of the monkfish tails.

2. Cut along the bone with a sharp filleting knife to separate the flesh from it.

3. Cut the monkfish into slices about 2.5cm/1 inch thick. Mix the salt and pepper with the flour and dredge the slices of monkfish, shaking off the excess. Fry in olive oil until golden brown. Remove and drain on paper towels.

4. Add the carrot and onion and fry gently for about 5 minutes. Add the bay leaf, parsley, vinegar, chilli pepper and 280ml/½ pint water. Cover and simmer gently for about 20 minutes.

5. Place the fish in a shallow casserole dish and pour over the marinade. Sprinkle on the sliced garlic and cover well. Refrigerate for 24 hours, turning the fish over several times.

6. To serve, remove the fish from the marinade and arrange on a serving plate. Pour the marinade on top of the fish and garnish with parsley, if desired.

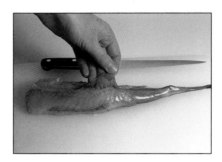

Step 1
Remove the brownish membrane from the outside of the monkfish tails.

Step 2
Using a sharp filleting knife, cut along the bone to separate one side of the tail. Repeat with the other side.

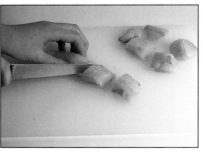

Step 3
Slice the tails into 2.5cm/1 inch thick pieces.

Cook's Notes

Time
Preparation takes about 25 minutes, with 24 hours refrigeration, cooking takes about 25 minutes.

Variation
Other fish, such as whole small trout or trout fillets or fish steaks such as cod or salmon, may be used.

Serving Ideas
Serve as a first course or for a light lunch with a salad and bread.

SERVES 4

PRAWN PASTRY PUFFS

These light pastry puffs are excellent savoury snacks for a
picnic or informal party.

90g/3oz butter
225ml/7 fl oz water
100g/3½oz plain flour, sieved
3 eggs, beaten
45g/1½oz butter
45g/1½oz flour
280ml/½ pint milk
2 tbsps white wine
1 bay leaf
180g/6oz peeled prawns, chopped
2 hard-boiled eggs, chopped
Pinch nutmeg
1 tsp chopped fresh dill
Salt and pepper

Step 2 Beat the
eggs vigorously
into the flour and
water mixture,
adding them
gradually, until a
smooth, shiny
paste is formed.

Step 6 Cut the
puffs almost in half
through the
middle and fill
each cavity with
the prawn and
egg mixture.

1. Put the 90g/3oz butter and the water into a saucepan.
Bring to the boil. Tip in the 100g/3½oz flour all at once and
beat, until the mixture is smooth and leaves the sides of the
pan clean. Leave to cool slightly.

2. Add the eggs gradually to the flour mixture, beating vigorously, until they are well incorporated and the mixture
forms a smooth, shiny paste.

3. Line a baking sheet with silicone paper and drop
heaped teaspoonsful of the mixture onto it, spaced well
apart. Bake in a preheated oven, 200°C/400°F/Gas Mark
6, for 25 minutes, or until the pastry puffs are firm to the
touch and golden brown.

4. Melt the remaining butter in a saucepan and stir in the
remaining flour. Blend in the milk gradually, beating well between additions. When all the milk is mixed in, add the wine
and bay leaf and bring to the boil, stirring constantly.

5. Remove the bay leaf and stir in the remaining
ingredients.

6. Cut the pastry puffs almost in half through the middle
and fill with the prawn and egg mixture.

Cook's Notes

 Time
Preparation will take about 15
minutes and cooking takes
about 30-35 minutes.

 Variation
Use wholemeal, instead of
plain white, flour to make the
pastry puffs.

 Preparation
The eggs can be mixed into
the flour and water mixture,
using a food mixer or processor.

Cook's Tip
To make sure that the pastry
puffs stay crisp, after cooking
is complete, make a small slit in the side
of each puff and return them to the
oven, with the heat switched off, for 5
minutes, so that they dry out
completely.

SERVES 4-8
CHILLED FISH CURRY

This sophisticated, mild curry will serve four as a refreshing summer lunch, or eight as an elegant starter.

225g/8oz fresh salmon fillet
350g/12oz whitefish fillet
Chicken stock
Salt and pepper
140ml/¼ pint mayonnaise
280ml/½ pint natural yogurt
2 tsps curry powder
Juice and grated rind of ½ lemon
120g/4oz peeled prawns

Garnish
Kiwi fruit, peeled and sliced
Sprigs fresh mint
Flaked coconut

1. Put the salmon and whitefish fillets into a shallow pan and add just enough chicken stock to cover.

2. Season to taste and simmer gently, until the fish is just tender.

3. Remove the fish carefully from the cooking liquor and

leave to cool slightly.

4. In a medium-sized bowl, mix together the mayonnaise and the yogurt. Blend in the curry powder and the lemon juice and rind.

5. Flake the cooked fish, removing any bones and skin. Mix the flaked fish into the curry sauce, together with the prawns.

6. Arrange the fish curry on serving plates and garnish with slices of kiwi fruit, sprigs of fresh mint and coconut flakes.

Step 4 Blend the curry powder and the lemon juice and rind thoroughly into the mayonnaise and yogurt mixture.

Step 1 Put the salmon and whitefish fillets into a shallow pan and pour over just enough chicken stock to cover.

Step 5 Flake the cooked fish, making sure that all skin and bones are removed.

Cook's Notes

Time
Preparation takes about 20 minutes, and cooking takes about 6 minutes.

Variation
If you prefer, use slices of peeled cucumber instead of the kiwi fruit.

Serving Ideas
Serve with boiled new potatoes or rice and a crisp mixed salad.

SERVES 4

FISH TEMPURA

This is a traditional Japanese dish, which can be served as
an unusual starter.

12 uncooked large prawns
2 whitefish fillets, skinned and cut into 5 x 2cm/
   2 x ¾-inch strips
Small whole fish, e.g. smelt or whitebait
2 squid, cleaned and cut into strips 2.5 x 7.5cm/1x3
   inches long
2 tbsps plain flour, for dusting
1 egg yolk
240ml/8 fl oz iced water
120g/4oz plain flour
Oil for frying
90ml/3 fl oz soy sauce
Juice and finely grated rind of 2 limes
60ml/2 fl oz dry sherry

1. Shell the prawns, leaving the tails intact. Wash the fish
and the squid and pat dry. Dust them all with the 2 tbsps
flour.

2. Make a batter by beating together the egg yolk and
water. Sieve in the 120g/4oz plain flour and mix in well with
a table knife.

Step 2 The batter
will be lumpy and
look under mixed.

3. Dip each piece of fish into the batter, shaking off any
excess.

4. In a wok or deep-fat fryer, heat the oil to 180°C/350°F.
Lower in the fish pieces a few at a time and cook for 2-3
minutes. Lift them out carefully and drain on paper towels,
keeping warm until required.

5. Mix together the soy sauce, lime juice, rind and sherry
and serve as a dip with the cooked fish.

Step 3 Do not
batter too many
pieces of fish at a
time. Only coat
those you are able
to cook.

Step 4 Cook only
3 or 4 pieces and
only one kind of
fish at a time.

Cook's Notes

Time
Preparation takes about 30
minutes and cooking time
varies from 2 to 3 minutes depending
on the type of fish.

Cook's Tip
If the batter seems to drain off
too quickly, leave each batch
of fish in the bowl of batter, until you are
ready to lower them into the hot oil.

Variation
Use a few vegetables, as well
as fish, for an interesting
change. Whole button mushrooms are
especially good.

SMOKED SALMON STUFFED CUCUMBERS

SERVES 4

This exquisite starter will soon become a firm favourite.

1 large cucumber
Salt for sprinkling
120g/4oz smoked salmon
180g/6oz curd cheese
2 tsps finely chopped fresh chives
140ml/¼ pint natural yogurt
2 tsps finely chopped fresh dill
2 tbsps whipping cream
Squeeze of lemon juice
Salt and pepper
1 head of iceberg lettuce
Red caviar, to garnish

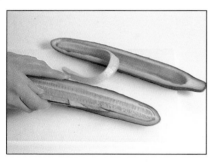

Step 1 Cut the cucumber in half lengthways and carefully scoop out the seeds using a serrated grapefruit spoon or knife.

1. Cut the cucumber in half lengthways and scoop out the seeds. Sprinkle the surface with salt and leave to stand for 1 hour.

2. Work the smoked salmon and the cheese in a blender until smooth. Stir in the chives.

3. Mix the yogurt, cream and dill together, adding lemon juice and seasoning to taste.

4. Rinse the cucumber thoroughly and pat as dry as possible. Using a pastry bag, fitted with a 1.5cm/½-inch plain nozzle, pipe the smoked salmon mixture into the hollow left in the cucumber, sandwich the two halves together firmly, wrap tightly in polythene or plastic wrap and chill for at least 1 hour.

5. Arrange the lettuce leaves on serving plates. Unwrap the cucumber, trim away the ends and slice carefully into 0.5cm/¼-inch slices. Arrange these on top of the lettuce.

6. Spoon a little of the yogurt mixture over, and garnish with a little red caviar.

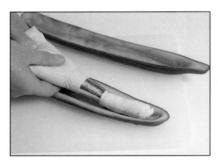

Step 4 Pipe the salmon mixture evenly in the hollow left in the cucumber by the removal of the seeds.

Step 5 Use a sharp knife to cut the chilled stuffed cucumber carefully into 0.5cm/¼-inch slices.

Cook's Notes

Time
Preparation takes about 15 minutes, but allow at least 1 hour for chilling, before serving.

Variation
Use halved, hard-boiled eggs, with the yolks removed, instead of the cucumber. The yolks can be sieved over the dressing instead of the caviar, if preferred.

Serving Ideas
Use the slices of stuffed cucumber, without the yogurt dressing, as part of a tray of hors d'oeuvres.

SERVES 4

SALMON PÂTÉ

This highly nutritious, elegant pâté is low in fat and very
quick to prepare.

225g/8oz canned red or pink salmon, drained
150g/5oz cup low fat curd cheese
Few drops lemon juice
Pinch ground mace, or ground nutmeg
¼ tsp Tabasco sauce
Freshly ground sea salt and black pepper
2 tbsps 1% fat fromage frais, or low fat natural yogurt
4 small pickles

1. Remove any bones and skin from the salmon. In a bowl,
work the fish into a smooth paste with the back of a spoon.

2. Beat the curd cheese until it is smooth.

3. Add the salmon, lemon juice, seasonings, and fromage
frais or natural yogurt to the curd cheese and mix well, until
thoroughly incorporated.

4. Divide the mixture equally between 4 individual custard
cups. Smooth the surfaces carefully.

5. Slice each pickle lengthways, 4 or 5 times, making sure
that you do not cut completely through the gherkin at the
narrow end. Splay the cut ends into a fan, and use these to

decorate the tops of the pâtés in the custard cups.

Step 1 Put the salmon into a small bowl and work it with the back of a spoon, until it becomes a smooth paste.

Step 5 Slice each pickle lengthways, 4 or 5 times, taking great care not to cut right through the pickle at the narrow end. Spread each of the cut ends out carefully into a fan shape. Use these to garnish the tops of the pâtés.

 *Cook's Notes*

 Time
Preparation takes about 15
minutes.

 Preparation
If you have a food processor or
liquidizer, you can work the
curd cheese and salmon together in
this, instead of beating them in a bowl.

 Variation
Use canned tuna fish in place
of the salmon, and stir in 1 tsp
horseradish sauce, instead of the
Tabasco sauce.

 Serving Ideas
Serve with toast, or crispy
wholemeal rolls.

SERVES 4

SCALLOPS IN SAFFRON SAUCE

Saffron is about the most expensive of all spices, but take
heart – only a few strands are needed in any recipe!

16 large scallops with coral attached
140ml/¼ pint water
140ml/¼ pint dry white wine
1 shallot, roughly chopped
1 bouquet garni, consisting of 1 bay leaf, 1 sprig of fresh
    thyme and 3 stalks of parsley
6 black peppercorns
A few strands of saffron
4 tbsps hot water
340ml/10 fl oz double cream
3 tbsps fresh chopped parsley
Salt and pepper

1. Put the scallops into a large shallow pan together with
the water, wine, shallot, bouquet garni and peppercorns.

2. Cover the pan and bring the liquid almost to the boil.
Remove the pan from the heat and leave the scallops to
poach in the hot liquid for 10-15 minutes.

3. The scallops are cooked when they are just firm to the
touch. Remove them from the liquid and keep warm on a
clean plate.

Step 1 Put the
scallops into a
large shallow pan,
along with the
water, wine,
shallot, bouquet
garni and
peppercorns.

4. Strain the scallop cooking liquid in a small saucepan
and bring to the boil. Allow the liquid to boil rapidly until it is
reduced by about half.

5. Soak the saffron in the hot water for about 5 minutes, or
until the colour has infused into the water.

6. Add the saffron with its soaking liquid, the double
cream and the chopped parsley to the reduced cooking
liquid and season to taste. Bring the sauce back to just
below boiling point.

7. Arrange the scallops on a serving plate and pour a little
of the sauce over them before serving.

Step 4 Reduce
the cooking liquid
by half by boiling
rapidly over a high
heat.

Step 5 Soak the
saffron in the hot
water for about 5
minutes, or until
the colour has
infused into the
water.

Cook's Notes

Time
Preparation takes about 15
minutes, and cooking also
takes about 15 minutes.

Preparation
If you do not wish to use
shellfish on the day you buy it,
it should be wrapped in newspaper and
stored in the bottom of the refrigerator
until the next day. It should not be kept
longer than overnight.

Serving Ideas
Serve as a starter with brown
bread and butter, or as a light
main course with rice or pasta.

SERVES 4

PRAWNS IN MELON

Deliciously cool and refreshing for a summer lunch,
this recipe could also be served as an unusual starter
for eight people.

2 small melons
4 medium tomatoes
1 small cucumber
1 orange
Juice of half a lemon
4 tbsps light vegetable oil
3 tbsps double cream
2 tbsps chopped fresh mint, reserve 4 sprigs for garnish
Pinch of sugar
Salt and pepper
1 tsp chopped fresh lemon thyme, optional
225g/8oz peeled prawns
90g/3oz toasted flaked almonds

Step 2 Prepare the fruit and vegetables so they are a convenient size to eat.

Step 3 Mix the dressing in a large bowl and add the rest of the ingredients to it, stirring well to coat thoroughly.

Step 1 Leave a 0.5cm/¼-inch border of flesh on the inside of each shell, so they are rigid enough to hold the salad.

1. Cut the melons in half through the middle, remove the seeds and scoop out the flesh with a melon baller, or spoon. Leave a 0.5cm/¼ -inch border of fruit on the inside of each shell.

2. Cut the melon flesh into 1cm/½-inch cubes, or leave in balls. Peel the tomatoes and remove the seeds. Cut the flesh into strips. Peel the cucumber, cut into half length-ways and then into 1cm/½-inch cubes. Peel and segment the orange.

3. In a large bowl, mix together the lemon juice, oil and double cream. Stir in the mint, sugar, salt and pepper and thyme, if using. Add the prawns and the fruit and vegetables, and mix thoroughly to coat evenly with the dressing.

4. Pile equal quantities of fruit and prawn mixture into the two shells and chill well.

5. Serve garnished with the reserved mint sprigs and the almonds.

Cook's Notes

Time
Preparation takes about 25 minutes. Allow at least 2 hours for chilling the salad, before serving.

Preparation
If the melon shells will not stand upright, cut a thin slice off the bottom of each one to make them more stable.

Serving Ideas
Serve with a mixed green salad and new potatoes.

SERVES 2-4

PRAWNS WITH MANGE TOUT

Snow peas, peapods and mangetout are
all names for the same vegetable – bright
green, crisp and edible, pods and all.

45ml/3 tbsps oil
60g/2oz split blanched almonds, halved
120g/4oz mange tout
60g/2oz bamboo shoots, sliced
10g/2 tsps cornflour
10ml/2 tsps light soy sauce
180ml/6 fl oz chicken stock
30ml/2 tbsps dry sherry
Salt and pepper
450g/1lb cooked, peeled prawns

Step 2 Tear stems downward to remove strings from mangetout.

1. Heat the oil in a wok. Add the almonds and cook over moderate heat until golden brown. Remove from the oil and drain on paper towels.

2. To prepare the mangetout, tear off the stems and pull them downwards to remove any strings. If the mangetout are small, just remove the stalks. Add the mangetout to the hot oil and cook for about 1 minute. Remove and set aside with the almonds.

3. Drain all the oil from the wok and mix together the cornflour and the remaining ingredients, except the prawns and bamboo shoots. Pour the mixture into the wok and stir constantly while bringing to the boil. Allow to simmer for 1-2 minutes until thickened and cleared. Stir in the prawns and all the other ingredients and heat through for about 1 minute. Serve immediately.

Step 2 If mangetout are very large, cut in half on the diagonal.

Step 3 Add all the ingredients to the wok and stir-fry, tossing with chopsticks or a fish slice.

Cook's Notes

Time
Preparation takes about 10 minutes, cooking takes 6-8 minutes.

Variation
If using spring onions, celery or water chestnuts, cook with the mangetout.

Watchpoint
Do not cook the prawns too long or on heat that is too high – they toughen quite easily.

Chapter II

SALADS

SERVES 4-6

CAESAR SALAD

A classic salad from the United States,
said to have been concocted one evening
from the only ingredients left in the kitchen.

6 anchovy fillets, soaked in 60ml/4 tbsps milk
280ml/½ pint olive oil
1 clove garlic, left whole
4 slices French bread, cut into 1.25cm/½" cubes
1 egg, cooked 1 minute
1 head Cos lettuce
Juice of 1 small lemon
Salt and pepper
60g/4 tbsps grated Parmesan cheese

Step 2 Fry the cubes of French bread in the hot oil, stirring them constantly for even browning.

1. Leave the anchovies to soak in the milk for 15 minutes. Rinse and pat dry on paper towels. Chop roughly.

2. Crush the garlic and leave in the oil for about 30 minutes. Heat all but 90ml/6 tbsps of the oil in a frying pan until hot. Fry the cubes of bread until golden brown, stirring constantly with a metal spoon for even browning. Drain on paper towels.

3. Break the cooked egg into a bowl and beat well with the lemon juice, salt and pepper. Toss the lettuce with the remaining garlic oil and anchovies. Add the egg mixture and toss to coat well. Place in a clean serving bowl and sprinkle over the croûtons and Parmesan cheese. Serve at room temperature.

Step 3 To make the dressing, break the egg into the bowl and mix well with the lemon juice and seasoning until slightly thickened.

Step 3 Add the oil to the lettuce separately and then toss with the egg dressing mixture.

Cook's Notes

Time
Preparation takes about 30 minutes and cooking takes about 3-5 minutes for the croûtons.

Cook's Tip
Soaking anchovy fillets in milk before using them neutralises the strong salty taste.

Watchpoint
Remove the croûtons from the hot fat when just barely brown enough. They continue to cook slightly in their own heat as they drain.

SERVES 4-6

PRAWN AND EGG SALAD

Serve this as a starter or a main course.
If desired, substitute more
vegetables for the prawns.

4 eggs
Half a bunch of spring onions, chopped
Half a small red pepper, chopped
Half a small green pepper, chopped
120g/4oz cooked, peeled prawns
1 small jar artichoke hearts, drained and quartered

Dressing

90ml/6 tbsps oil
30ml/2 tbsps white wine vinegar
1 clove garlic, finely chopped
5ml/1 tsp dry mustard
2.5ml/½ tsp hot red pepper flakes
Salt

1. Prick the large end of the eggs with an egg pricker or a needle.

2. Lower each egg carefully into boiling, salted water. Bring the water back to the boil, rolling the eggs in the water with the bowl of a spoon.

3. Cook the eggs for 9 minutes once the water comes back to the boil. Drain and rinse under cold water until completely cool. Peel and quarter. Combine the eggs with the other ingredients in a large bowl.

4. Mix the dressing ingredients together using a whisk to get a thick emulsion.

5. Pour the dressing over the salad and mix carefully so that the eggs do not break up.

6. Serve on beds of shredded lettuce, if desired.

Step 2 Lower each egg carefully into the water and roll around with the bowl of a spoon to set the yolk.

Step 4 Mix the dressing ingredients together using a whisk to get a thick emulsion.

Cook's Notes

Time
Preparation takes about 25 minutes and cooking takes about 9 minutes to boil the eggs.

Preparation
If preparing the eggs in advance, leave in the shells and in cold water. This will prevent a grey ring forming around the yolks.

Cook's Tip
Rolling the eggs around in the hot water helps to set the yolk in the centre of the white and makes sliced or quartered eggs more attractive.

SERVES 4-6

SUMMER SEAFOOD SALAD

This impressive salad is simple to prepare.

450g/1lb cooked, peeled prawns
450g/1lb seedless white grapes, halved if large
6 sticks celery, thinly sliced on diagonal
100g/4oz toasted flaked almonds
100g/4oz canned water chestnuts, sliced or diced
225g/8oz canned lychees
1 small fresh pineapple, peeled, cored and cut into
   pieces
280ml/10fl oz mayonnaise
1 tbsp honey
1 tbsp light soy sauce
2 tbsps mild curry powder
Juice of half a lime
Chinese cabbage or Belgian endive

Step 1 Trim the point of each quarter of pineapple to remove the core.

1. Combine the prawns, grapes, celery, almonds, water chestnuts and lychees in a large bowl. Trim off the top and bottom of the pineapple and quarter. Slice off the points of each quarter to remove the core.

Step 2 Use a serrated fruit knife to slice between the skin and pineapple flesh.

2. Slice the pineapple skin away and cut the flesh into bite-size pieces. Add to the prawns and toss to mix.

3. Break the Chinese cabbage or endive and wash well. If using Chinese cabbage, shred the leafy part finely, saving the thicker ends of the leaves for other use. Place the Chinese cabbage on salad plates. Mix the remaining dressing ingredients thoroughly. Pile the salad ingredients onto the leaves and spoon over some of the dressing, leaving the ingredients showing. Separate endive leaves and arrange them whole. Serve remaining dressing separately.

Step 2 Add pineapple pieces to the prawns and mix well.

Cook's Notes

Time
Preparation takes about 30 minutes.

Serving Ideas
Serve as a main course salad for lunch or a light dinner. Serve in smaller quantities as a starter.

Variation
Other seafood may be substituted for the prawns. Use crab, lobster or shellfish such as mussels.

SERVES 4

PRAWN REMOULADE

The prawns in this dish 'cook' in the refrigerator in a marinade that is piquant with mustard, horseradish and wine vinegar.

1½lbs raw unshelled large prawns
45g/3 tbsps mild mustard
10g/2 tsps horseradish
1 tbsp paprika
1 fresh chilli pepper, seeded and finely chopped
1 clove garlic, crushed
Salt
100ml/4fl oz white wine vinegar
300ml/12fl oz oil
6 spring onions, sliced
2 sticks celery, thinly sliced
2 bay leaves
2 tbsps chopped parsley
Lettuce and lemon wedges

1. Shell the prawns, except for the very tail ends. If desired, the prawns may be completely shelled.

2. Combine the mustard, horseradish, paprika, chilli pepper, garlic and salt in a deep bowl. Mix in the vinegar thoroughly.

3. Add the oil in a thin, steady stream while beating constantly with a small whisk. Continue to beat until the sauce is smooth and thick. Add the spring onions, celery, bay leaves and chopped parsley. Cover the bowl tightly and leave in the refrigerator for several hours, or overnight.

4. Two hours before serving, add the prawns to the marinade and stir to coat them well. Leave in the refrigerator until ready to serve.

5. To serve, shred the lettuce finely and place on individual serving plates. Arrange the prawns on top and spoon over some of the marinade to serve, discarding the bay leaves.

Step 2 Combine marinade ingredients in a bowl and stir in the vinegar.

Step 3 Using a small whisk, gradually blend in the oil until the sauce is smooth and thick.

Step 4 Add the prawns to the marinade and stir well to coat.

Cook's Notes

Time
Preparation takes about 25 minutes plus overnight chilling for the marinade and 2 hours marinating time for the prawns.

Cook's Tip
After two hours' marinating the seafood will look cooked, that is opaque and slightly firm. However, it is still raw, so absolutely fresh seafood is required.

Variation
Scallops, quartered or sliced, depending on the size, mussels, clams or whitefish, cut into thin strips, may be used instead of or in addition to the prawns.

SERVES 4

DRESSED CRAB SALAD

The rosy hued dressing is both creamy and
piquant – perfect for crab meat.

2 large cooked crabs
1 head iceberg lettuce
4 large tomatoes
4 hard-boiled eggs
16 black olives
280ml/½ pint prepared mayonnaise
60ml/4 tbsps whipping cream
60ml/4 tbsps chilli sauce or tomato chutney
½ green pepper, seeded and finely diced
3 spring onions, finely chopped
Salt and pepper

1. To prepare the crabs, break off the claws and set them aside. Turn the crabs over and press up with thumbs to separate the body from the shell of each.

2. Cut the body into quarters and use a skewer to pick out the white meat. Discard the stomach sac and the lungs (dead-man's fingers). Scrape out the brown meat from the shell to use, if desired.

3. Crack the large claws and legs and remove the meat. Break into shreds, discarding any shell or cartilage.

Combine all the meat and set it aside.

4. Shred the lettuce finely, quarter the tomatoes and chop the eggs.

5. Combine the mayonnaise, cream, chilli sauce or chutney, green pepper and spring onions and mix well.

6. Arrange the shredded lettuce on serving plates and divide the crab meat evenly.

7. Spoon some of the dressing over each serving of crab and sprinkle with the chopped egg. Garnish each serving with tomato wedges and olives and serve the remaining dressings separately.

Step 1 Turn crabs over and press up with thumbs to separate the under-body from the shell.

Cook's Notes

Time
Preparation takes about 30-40 minutes.

Preparation
To shred lettuce finely, break off the leaves and stack them up a few at a time. Use a large, sharp knife to cut across the leaves into thin shreds.

Variation
Frozen crab meat may be used instead of fresh. Make sure it is completely defrosted and well drained before using. Pick through the meat to remove any bits of shell or cartilage left behind.

SERVES 4

SPANISH RICE AND SOLE SALAD

A complete meal in itself, this salad
is ideal for a summer lunch.

2 large lemon sole, each filleted into 4 pieces
4-6 peppercorns
Slice of onion
1 tbsp lemon juice
175g/6oz cup long grain rice
1 small aubergine
2 tbsps olive oil
1 red pepper, seeded and chopped into 0.5cm/¼-inch
 dice
1 shallot, finely chopped
1 green pepper, seeded and chopped into 0.5cm/
 ¼-inch dice
3 tbsps French dressing
1 tbsp chopped fresh mixed herbs
280ml/½ pint prepared mayonnaise
1 clove garlic, crushed
1 level tsp tomato purée
1 level tsp paprika
Salt and pepper
2 bunches watercress, to garnish

Step 1 Allow the fish to cool, then cut each fillet into 2.5cm/1-inch pieces.

Step 4 Mix the aubergine into the rice along with the peppers.

1. Lay the sole fillets in an ovenproof dish, together with the peppercorns, slice of onion, lemon juice and just enough water to cover. Sprinkle with a little salt and cover the dish with foil or a lid. Poach in a preheated oven, 180°C/350°F/Gas Mark 4, for 8-10 minutes. Allow the fish to cool in the liquor, then cut each fillet into 1-inch pieces.

2. Cook the rice in boiling water, until soft. Rinse in cold water and separate the grains with a fork.

3. Cut the aubergine in half and sprinkle with 2 tsps salt. Allow to stand for ½ an hour, then rinse very thoroughly. Pat dry and cut into 2.5cm/1-inch dice.

4. Heat the oil in a large frying pan, and fry the aubergine, until it is soft. Allow the aubergine to cool, then mix it into the rice along with the shallot, peppers, half the chopped herbs and the French dressing.

5. Mix together the mayonnaise, garlic, tomato purée, paprika, remaining herbs and seasoning.

6. Arrange the rice on one side of a serving dish and the sole pieces on the other. Spoon the mayonnaise over the sole and garnish the dish with watercress.

Cook's Notes

Time
Preparation will take about 20 minutes. Cooking takes about 15-20 minutes.

Cook's Tip
Cooked rice usually weighs about twice its dry weight.

Freezing
Rice can be cooked and frozen in convenient amounts. To use, the frozen rice should be put straight into boiling water and allowed to cook for 3-4 minutes, then rinsed in cold water.

SERVES 4

SEVICHE

Do not be put off by the thought of eating raw fish, as the cod will 'cook' in the spicy marinade and the result is absolutely delicious.

450g/1lb cod fillets
Juice and grated rind of 2 limes
1 shallot, chopped
1 green chilli pepper, seeded and finely chopped
1 tsp ground coriander
1 small green pepper, seeded and sliced
1 small red pepper, seeded and sliced
1 tbsp chopped fresh parsley
1 tbsp chopped fresh coriander leaves
4 green olives, chopped
2 tbsps olive oil
Salt and pepper
1 small lettuce

Step 2 Stir the lime juice and rind, together with the shallot and spices, into the strips of cod, mixing thoroughly to coat them evenly with the spice mixture.

Step 4 Stir the peppers, herbs, onion and oil into the drained fish.

Step 1 Cut the skinned cod fillets into thin strips across the grain, removing any bones you may find.

1. Skin the cod fillets and cut them into thin strips across the grain.

2. Put the cod strips into a bowl, pour over the lime juice

and rind. Add the shallot, chilli pepper and coriander, and stir well to coat the fish completely.

3. Cover the bowl and refrigerate for 24 hours, stirring occasionally.

4. When ready to serve, drain the fish and stir in the peppers, parsley, coriander leaves, onions and oil. Season to taste and serve on a bed of lettuce.

Cook's Notes

Time
Preparation takes about 20 minutes, plus 24 hours refrigeration.

Variation
Substitute haddock or monkfish fillets for the cod.

Serving Ideas
Serve with crusty French bread or tortilla chips.

SERVES 4

PRAWNS AND CASHEWS IN PINEAPPLE WITH TARRAGON DRESSING

Served in the pineapple shells, this impressive salad is ideal
for a summer lunch or buffet.

2 small fresh pineapples, with nice green tops
225g/8oz cooked, peeled prawns
120g/4oz roasted, unsalted cashew nuts
2 sticks of celery, thinly sliced
4 tbsps lemon juice
1 egg
2 tbsps caster sugar
1 tbsp tarragon vinegar
2 tsps chopped fresh tarragon
120ml/4 fl oz whipping cream

1. Cut the pineapples carefully in half lengthways, leaving their green tops attached.

2. Cut out the pineapple flesh carefully, leaving a 5mm/¼-inch border of flesh on the inside of the shell. Remove the cores and cut the flesh into bite-sized pieces.

3. Put the chopped pineapple into a bowl, along with the prawns, cashew nuts and celery. Pour in the lemon juice and mix well. Divide the mixture equally between the pineapple shells, and chill them in the refrigerator.

4. In a heat-proof bowl, whisk together the egg and sugar. Stand the bowl over a pan of simmering water, and whisk in the vinegar and tarragon. Continue whisking until the mixture has thickened.

5. Remove the bowl from the heat and allow to cool completely, whisking occasionally.

6. When completely cold, whip the cream until it is just beginning to thicken, then fold it into the dressing mixture.

7. Pour the cream dressing over the salad in the pineapple shells and serve.

Step 1 Cut the pineapples in half lengthways, making sure that the leafy tops stay intact.

Step 4 Whisk the egg and sugar mixture, together with the vinegar and the tarragon, over a pan of simmering water, until it is pale and thick.

Step 6 Fold the lightly whipped cream carefully into the tarragon and egg dressing, before pouring it over the individual salads.

Cook's Notes

Time
Preparation takes about 30 minutes, and cooking about 10–15 minutes.

Preparation
Whisking the egg and sugar dressing can be done with an electric mixer. It will not then be necessary to whisk the dressing over a pan of hot water.

Cook's Tip
If you cannot buy unsalted cashew nuts, wash salted ones in water, but make sure they are completely dry before adding them to the salad.

SERVES 4

VINEGARED CRAB

An unusual way of serving fresh crab. You should be able to buy the rice vinegar from a delicatessen or health food shop. If not, substitute white wine vinegar.

1 small cucumber, grated
Salt, for sprinkling
1 large cooked crab
1 small piece fresh ginger, grated
Chinese cabbage, for serving
3 tbsps rice vinegar
2 tbsps dry sherry
2 tbsps soy sauce

1. Sprinkle the cucumber with salt and leave for 30 minutes.

2. Crack the legs and claws off the crab. Remove the meat from the claws and legs, but leave four thin legs whole as a garnish.

3. Separate the underbody from the shell. Remove and discard the stomach sac and the grey, feathered gills.

4. Scrape the brown meat from the shell and crack open the underbody. Use a skewer to pick out the meat.

5. Rinse the cucumber, drain well and squeeze out excess moisture. Mix together the cucumber, crab meat and ginger.

6. Arrange the Chinese cabbage on serving plates, to represent crab shells. Pile equal quantities of crab mixture onto the Chinese cabbage, leaving some of the leaf showing. Garnish with a whole crab leg and some grated, pickled ginger, if you can get it.

7. Mix together the vinegar, sherry and soy sauce. Serve with the crab in little bowls.

Step 2 Remove meat from claws and legs.

Step 4 Crack open the underbody of the crab and use a skewer to remove the white meat inside.

Cook's Notes

Time
Preparation takes about 30 minutes.

Cook's Tip
When choosing a fresh crab, select one which feels heavy for its size and inside which, when shaken, no water can be heard.

Serving Ideas
A rice or pasta salad would be excellent with this dish.

SERVES 6

LOBSTER AND CAULIFLOWER SALAD

This salad has a touch of elegance that makes it the sophisticated choice for a stylish meal.

1 large cauliflower, washed
140ml/¼ pint vegetable oil
3 tbsps lemon juice
1 tbsp dry mustard
Salt and pepper
1 large cooked lobster
280ml/½ pint mayonnaise
2 tsps Dijon mustard
4 hard-boiled eggs, coarsely chopped
16 black olives, halved and pitted
2 bunches watercress, washed
Red caviar

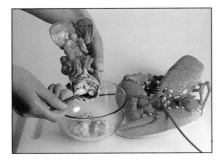

Step 2 Crack open the lobster and pick out all the meat from the shell and claws.

Step 1 Coat the cauliflower florets thoroughly with the oil, lemon juice and dry mustard, before marinating it for at least 2 hours.

1. Break the cauliflower into small florets and mix with the oil, lemon juice, dry mustard and seasoning, stirring well, to ensure that all the cauliflower is well coated. Chill for at least 2 hours.

2. Crack the lobster and remove all the meat from the shell and claws. Put the lobster meat into a bowl and stir in the mayonnaise and Dijon mustard.

3. Mix the eggs and olives into the cauliflower, tossing gently so as not to break up the eggs.

4. Trim the watercress and arrange it on a serving plate. Spoon over the cauliflower mixture and top with the lobster and mayonnaise mixture. Sprinkle with the caviar and serve at once.

Cook's Notes

Time
Preparation takes about 30 minutes.

Variation
Fresh crab could be used instead of the lobster, to make an equally delicious dish.

Serving Ideas
Serve with small new potatoes and well-chilled white wine.

Chapter III

EVERYDAY DISHES

SERVES 2

BARBECUED PRAWNS

It's the sauce rather than the cooking method that
gives the dish its name. It's spicy, zippy and *hot*.

450g/1lb large prawns, cooked and unpeeled
100g/4oz unsalted butter
1 tsp each white, black and cayenne pepper
Pinch salt
1 tsp each chopped fresh thyme, rosemary and
 marjoram
1 clove garlic, crushed
1 tsp Worcester sauce
125ml/5fl oz fish stock
60ml/4 tbsps dry white wine
Cooked rice

Remove the prawns and set them aside.

3. Add the Worcester sauce, stock and wine to the
ingredients in the pan. Bring to the boil and cook for about
3 minutes to reduce. Add salt to taste.

4. Arrange the prawns on a bed of rice and pour over the
sauce to serve.

Step 2 Melt the butter and add the spices, herbs and prawns, and cook briefly.

Step 1 Remove the legs and eyes from the prawns. Leave on the long antennae, if desired.

Step 3 Add the Worcester sauce, wine and stock to the pan and boil rapidly to reduce.

1. Remove the eyes and the legs from the prawns.

2. Melt the butter in a large frying pan and add the white
pepper, black pepper, cayenne pepper, herbs and garlic.
Add the prawns and toss over heat for a few minutes.

Cook's Notes

Time
Preparation takes about 15
minutes and cooking takes
about 5 mintues.

Preparation
Because the prawns are pre-
cooked, cook them very
briefly again, just to heat through. Use
uncooked, unpeeled prawns if
possible. Cook these until they curl and
turn pink.

Serving Ideas
The prawns may also be
served cold. If serving cold,
prepare the sauce with 6 tbsps oil
instead of the butter.

SERVES 6

SEAFOOD STEW

This makes the most of the delicious
and varied fish and shellfish found
off Spain's beautiful coastline.

24 clams or mussels in the shell
3 squid
900g/2lb firm whitefish, filleted into 5cm/2 inch pieces
3 medium-sized tomatoes, peeled, seeded and chopped
½ green pepper, seeded and chopped
1 small onion, chopped
1 clove garlic, finely chopped
280ml/½ pint dry white wine
Salt and pepper
140ml/¼ pint olive oil
6 slices French bread
45ml/3 tbsps chopped parsley

1. Scrub the clams or mussels well to remove the beards and barnacles. Discard any shellfish with broken shells or ones that do not close when tapped. Place the mussels or clams in a large saucepan or heatproof casserole, scatter over about half of the vegetables and garlic and spoon over 60ml/4 tbsps of the olive oil.

2. To clean the squid, hold the tail section in one hand and the head section in the other to pull the tail away from the head.

3. Cut the tentacles free from the head just above the eyes. Discard the head, entrails and ink sack.

4. Remove the quill from the body of the squid and peel away the reddish-purple outer skin.

5. Slice the tail into strips about 1.25cm/½ inch thick. Cut the tentacles into individual pieces.

6. Scatter the squid and the prepared whitefish over the vegetables in the pan and top with the remaining vegetables. Pour over the white wine and season with salt and

pepper. Bring to the boil over high heat and then reduce to simmering. Cover the pan and cook for about 20 minutes or until the clams open, the squid is tender and the fish flakes easily. Discard any clams or mussels that do not open.

7. Heat the remaining olive oil in a frying pan and when hot, add the slices of bread, browning them well on both sides. Drain on paper towels.

8. Place a slice of bread in the bottom of a soup bowl and ladle the fish mixture over the bread. Sprinkle with parsley and serve immediately.

Step 2
To clean the squid, separate the head from the tail by pulling them in opposite directions

Step 4
Remove the quill from the tail and peel the reddish-purple skin from the outside.

Cook's Notes

Time
Preparation takes about 35 minutes and cooking takes about 20 minutes.

Preparation
Fry the bread while the fish stew is cooking. The stew must be served immediately and not reheated.

Variation
Different kinds of fish, such as haddock, cod, halibut or sea bass can be used.

SERVES 4

PLAICE WITH SPICY TOMATO SAUCE

This piquant fish dish is popular along
Mexico's Gulf coast.

90g/3oz cream cheese
5ml/1 tsp dried oregano
Pinch cayenne pepper
4 whole fillets of plaice
Lime slices and dill to garnish

Tomato Sauce

15ml/1 tbsp oil
1 small onion, chopped
1 stick celery, chopped
1 chilli pepper, seeded and chopped
1.25ml/¼ tsp each ground cumin, coriander and ginger
½ red and ½ green pepper, seeded and chopped
400g/14oz canned tomatoes
15ml/1 tbsp tomato purée
Salt, pepper and a pinch sugar

1. Heat the oil in a heavy-based pan and cook the onion, celery, chilli pepper and spices for about 5 minutes over very low heat.

2. Add red and green peppers and the remaining ingredients and bring to the boil. Reduce heat and simmer 15-20 minutes, stirring occasionally. Set aside while preparing the fish.

3. Mix the cream cheese, oregano and cayenne pepper together and set aside.

4. Skin the fillets using a filleting knife. Start at the tail end and hold the knife at a slight angle to the skin.

5. Push the knife along using a sawing motion, with the blade against the skin. Dip fingers in salt to make it easier to hold onto the fish skin. Gradually separate the fish from the skin.

6. Spread the cheese filling on all 4 fillets and roll each up. Secure with cocktail sticks.

7. Place the fillets in a lightly greased baking dish, cover and cook for 10 minutes in a preheated 180°C/350°F/Gas Mark 4 oven.

8. Pour over the tomato sauce and cook a further 10-15 minutes. Fish is cooked when it feels firm and looks opaque. Garnish with lime slices and dill.

Step 5 Using a filleting knife held at an angle, push the knife along, cutting against the fish skin. Use a sawing motion to separate flesh from skin.

Step 6 Spread cheese filling on the fish and roll up each fillet.

Cook's Notes

Time
Preparation takes about 30 minutes and cooking takes 20-25 minutes.

Serving Ideas
Add rice and an avocado salad.

Special Occasions
Add prawns or crabmeat to the filling for a dinner party dish.

SERVES 6

CHILLI PRAWN QUICHE

Fresh chilli peppers give a Mexican flavour
to this quiche with its prawn filling.

Pastry

120g/4oz plain flour
Pinch salt
30g/2 tbsps butter or margarine
30g/2 tbsps white cooking fat
30-60ml/2-4 tbsps cold water

Filling

4 eggs
140ml/¼ pint milk
140ml/¼ pint single cream
½ clove garlic, crushed
120g/4oz Cheddar cheese, grated
3 spring onions, chopped
2 green chillies, seeded and chopped
225g/8oz cooked and peeled prawns
Salt
Cooked, unpeeled prawns and parsley sprigs for garnish

1. Sift the flour with a pinch of salt into a mixing bowl, or place in a food processor and mix once or twice.

2. Rub in the butter and fat until the mixture resembles fine breadcrumbs, or work in the food processor, being careful not to over-mix.

3. Mix in the liquid gradually, adding enough to bring the pastry together into a ball. In a food processor, add the liquid through the funnel while the machine is running.

4. Wrap the pastry well and chill for 20-30 minutes.

5. Roll out the pastry on a well-floured surface with a floured rolling pin.

6. Wrap the circle of pastry around the rolling pin to lift it into a 25cm/10 inch flan dish. Unroll the pastry over the dish.

7. Carefully press the pastry onto the bottom and up the sides of the dish, taking care not to stretch it.

8. Roll the rolling pin over the top of the dish to remove excess pastry, or cut off with a sharp knife.

9. Mix the eggs, milk, cream and garlic together. Sprinkle the cheese, onion, chillies and prawns onto the base of the pastry and pour over the egg mixture.

10. Bake in a preheated 200°C/400°F/Gas Mark 6 oven for 30-40 minutes until firm and golden brown. Peel the tail shells off the prawns and remove the legs and roe if present. Use to garnish the quiche along with the sprigs of parsley.

Step 6 Use the rolling pin to help lift the pastry into the flan dish.

Step 7 Carefully press the pastry into the dish to line the base and sides.

Cook's Notes

Time
Preparation takes about 40 minutes, which includes time for the pastry to chill. Cooking takes 30-40 minutes.

Variation
Add diced red or green peppers and chopped coriander leaves to the filling before baking.

Serving Ideas
Serve as a starter, cut in thin wedges or baked in individual dishes. Serve hot or cold with a salad for a snack or light meal.

SERVES 4-6

FISHERMAN'S STEW

This quick, economical and satisfying
fish dish will please any fish lover
for lunch or a light supper.

90ml/6 tbsps olive oil
2 large onions, sliced
1 red pepper, seeded and sliced
120g/4oz mushrooms, sliced
450g/1lb canned tomatoes
Pinch salt and pepper
Pinch dried thyme
430ml/¾ pint water
900g/2lb white fish fillets, skinned
140ml/¼ pint white wine
30ml/2 tbsps chopped parsley

1. Heat the oil in a large saucepan and add the onions. Cook until beginning to look transluscent. Add the pepper and cook until the vegetables are softened.

2. Add the mushrooms and the tomatoes and bring the mixture to the boil.

3. Add thyme, salt, pepper and water and simmer for about 30 minutes.

4. Add the fish and wine and cook until the fish flakes easily, about 15 minutes. Stir in parsley.

5. To serve, place a piece of toasted French bread in the bottom of the soup bowl and spoon over the fish stew.

Use a sharp knife to cut the onion into thin cross-ways slices.

Step 1 Cook the onions in the oil along with the peppers until soft.

Cook's Notes

 Time
Preparation takes about 20 minutes and cooking takes about 45 minutes.

 Variation
Shellfish may be added with the fish, if desired. Substitute green peppers for red peppers.

Serving Ideas
The stew may also be served over rice. Accompany with a green salad.

BUTTERED PRAWNS

This make a rich starter or an
elegant main course, yet it's
surprisingly easy.

900g/2lbs cooked prawns
60g/2oz butter, softened
Pinch salt, white pepper and cayenne
1 clove garlic, crushed
90g/6 tbsps fine dry breadcrumbs
30g/2 tbsps chopped parsley
60ml/4 tbsps sherry
Lemon wedges or slices

Step 2 Pull off the
tail shell and
carefully remove
the very end.

Step 1 Remove
the heads and
legs from the
prawns first.
Remove any roe
at this time.

Step 6 Spread the
mixture to
completely cover
the prawns.

1. To prepare the prawns, remove the heads and legs first.

2. Peel off the shells, carefully removing the tail shells.

3. Remove the black vein running down the length of the rounded side with a cocktail stick. If desired, peeled prawns may be used instead.

4. Arrange prawns in a shallow casserole or individual dishes.

5. Combine the remaining ingredients, except the lemon garnish, mixing well.

6. Spread the mixture to completely cover the prawns and place in a pre-heated 190°C/375°F Gas Mark 5 oven for about 20 minutes, or until the butter melts and the crumbs become crisp. Garnish with lemon wedges or slices.

Cook's Notes

 Time
Preparation takes about 35-40
minutes and cooking takes
about 20 minutes.

£ **Buying Guide**
Freshly cooked prawns are
available from most
fishmongers. Substitute frozen prawns,
if necessary.

SERVES 4

GRILLED FLOUNDER

A mayonnaise-like topping puffs
to a golden brown to give this mild-
flavoured fish a piquant taste.

4 double fillets of flounder
2 eggs, separated
Pinch salt, pepper and dry mustard
250ml/9fl oz peanut oil
60g/4 tbsps pickle
1 tbsp chopped parsley
1 tbsp lemon juice
Dash Tabasco

1. Place the egg yolks in a blender, food processor or deep bowl.

2. Blend in the salt, pepper and mustard. If blending by hand, use a small whisk.

3. If using the machine, pour the oil through the funnel in a thin, steady stream with the machine running. If mixing by hand, add oil a few drops at a time, beating well in between each addition.

4. When half the oil has been added, the rest may be added in a thin steady stream while beating constantly with a small whisk.

5. Mix in the relish, parsley, lemon juice and Tabasco. Beat the egg whites until stiff but not dry and fold into the mayonnaise.

6. Grill the fish about 2 inches from the heat source for about 6-10 minutes, depending on the thickness of the fillets.

7. Spread the sauce over each fillet and grill for 3-5 minutes longer, or until the sauce puffs and browns lightly.

Step 4 Add the oil to the egg yolk mixture in a thin, steady stream while beating constantly.

Step 5 Fold stiffly-beaten egg whites thoroughly into the mayonnaise.

Step 7 Spread or spoon the sauce over each fish fillet before grilling.

Cook's Notes

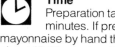 **Time**
Preparation takes about 20 minutes. If preparing the mayonnaise by hand this will take about 15-20 minutes. The fish takes 9-15 minutes to cook.

 Watchpoint
When preparing the mayonnaise either by machine or by hand, do not add the oil too quickly or the mayonnaise will curdle. If it does curdle, beat another egg yolk in a bowl and gradually beat in the curdled mixture. This should bring it back together again.

 Variation
This same topping may be used on other fish besides flounder.

 Serving Ideas
Serve with grilled tomatoes.

SERVES 4

FRIED BASS IN CORNMEAL

As a coating for frying, cornmeal is
superb. It fries to a crisp crunch
and adds subtle flavour of its own.

2lb freshwater bass or other whitefish fillets
Milk
500g/18fl oz yellow cornmeal
2 tbsps flour
Pinch salt
2 tsps cayenne pepper
1 tsp ground cumin
2 tsps garlic granules
Lime wedges to garnish

Step 3 Mix the cornmeal coating on a sheet of wax paper, place on the fish and lift the ends to toss and coat.

Step 2 Dip the fillets into milk and then hold by one end to allow the excess to drip off.

Step 5 Turn the fish over once it floats to the surface of the oil.

1. Mix the cornmeal, flour, salt, cayenne, cumin and garlic together in a shallow container or on a piece of wax paper.

2. Skin the fillets if desired. Dip them into the milk and then lift to allow the excess to drip off.

3. Place the fish in the cornmeal mixture and turn with two forks or, if using paper, lift the ends and toss the fish to coat.

4. Meanwhile, heat oil in a deep frying pan, large saucepan or deep fat fryer.

5. Add the fish in small batches and cook until the fillets float to the surface. Turn over and cook to brown lightly and evenly.

6. Drain on paper towels and serve immediately with lime wedges.

Cook's Notes

Time
Preparation takes about 20 minutes and cooking takes about 5 minutes per batch of fish.

Serving Ideas
Red pepper preserves or hot pepper relish may be served as a condiment with this fish.

Variation
If substituting another type of fish for bass, make sure that it is a firm-fleshed fish.

SERVES 4
GRILLED FISH WITH ROMESCU

Romescu is a sauce that evolved from a fish stew recipe
and is still often considered a dish on its own. It is
simple to make and has a strong, pungent taste.

900g/2lbs whole fish such as trout, red mullet, herring,
  sardines or mackerel, allowing 1-4 fish per person,
  depending on size.
Bay leaves
Salt and pepper
Olive oil
Lemon juice

Romescu (Almond and Hot Pepper Sauce)

1 tomato, peeled, seeded and chopped
45g/3 tbsps ground almonds
½ clove garlic, crushed
2.5ml/½ tsp cayenne pepper
Pinch salt
45ml/3 tbsps red wine vinegar
180ml/6 fl oz olive oil

Step 1
Mix all the
ingredients
together into a
smooth paste
using a mortar
and pestle.

1. To prepare the sauce, combine all the ingredients,
except the olive oil and vinegar, in a mortar and pestle and
work to a smooth mixture.

2. Transfer to a bowl, whisk in red wine vinegar and add
the oil gradually, a few drops at a time, mixing vigorously
with a wire whisk or a wooden spoon. Make sure each
addition of oil is absorbed before adding more. Once about
half the oil is added, the remainder may be poured in in a
thin, steady stream. Adjust the seasoning and set the sauce
aside.

3. Wash the fish well, sprinkle the cavities with salt and
pepper and place in a bay leaf. Brush the skin with olive oil
and sprinkle with lemon juice. Place under a preheated grill
and cook for about 2-5 minutes per side, depending on the
thickness of the fish. Brush with lemon juice and olive oil
while the fish is grilling. Serve with the sauce and lemon or
lime wedges if desired.

Step 2
Transfer the paste
to a bowl and
whisk in the wine
vinegar.

Step 2
Once half the oil
has been added,
add the remain-
der in a thin,
steady stream,
whisking by hand.

Cook's Notes

Time
Preparation takes about 20
minutes and cooking takes
about 10-20 minutes.

Preparation
The sauce may be made
several days in advance and
stored tightly sealed in the refrigerator.
Allow the sauce to come to room
temperature and whisk again before
serving.

Serving Ideas
Serve with boiled or fried
potatoes and a salad.

SERVES 4

FISH, COURGETTE AND LEMON KEBABS

Ask your fishmonger to fillet and skin the sole for you if you
feel that you cannot do it yourself.

16 small, thin sole fillets, or 8 larger ones, skinned and
   cut in half lengthways
4 tbsps olive oil
1 clove garlic, crushed
Juice ½ lemon
Finely grated rind ½ lemon
Freshly ground sea salt and black pepper, to taste
3 drops Tabasco sauce
2 medium-sized courgettes, cut into 5mm/¼-inch slices
1 green pepper, halved, seeded and cut into
   2.5mm/1-inch pieces

1. Roll up each sole fillet like a Swiss roll and secure with a cocktail stick.

2. Place the fish rolls in a shallow dish. Mix together the olive oil, garlic, lemon juice, lemon rind, salt and pepper and Tabasco sauce.

3. Spoon the olive oil mixture evenly over fish rolls, and chill for about 2 hours.

4. Remove the cocktail sticks, and carefully thread the rolled fish fillets onto kebab skewers alternately with the courgette slices and pieces of green pepper.

5. Brush each threaded kebab with a little of the lemon and oil marinade.

6. Arrange the kebab skewers on a grill pan and cook under a moderately hot grill for about 8 minutes, carefully turning the kebabs once or twice during cooking and brushing them with a little of the remaining marinade, if required.

Step 1 Roll up each sole fillet like a Swiss roll, from a narrow end, and secure each roll with a cocktail stick.

Step 4 Thread the rolled fish onto kebab skewers alternately with a courgette slice and pieces of green pepper.

Cook's Notes

Time
Preparation takes about 30 minutes, plus 2 hours chilling time, and cooking takes about 8 minutes.

Cook's Tip
The marinade ingredients are delicious used with other types of fish.

Variation
If sole is not in season, substitute small dab or plaice.

Serving Ideas
Serve the kebabs on a bed of brown rice, sprinkled with chopped parsley.

SERVES 4

COD IN PAPRIKA SAUCE

Creamy paprika sauce complements the flavour of cod
magnificently in this tasty recipe.

450g/1lb cod fillets
Lemon juice
1 bay leaf
Slice of onion
6 peppercorns
2 tbsps butter
60g/2oz button mushrooms, trimmed and sliced
1 small red pepper, seeded and sliced
1 shallot, finely chopped
2 tsps paprika pepper
1 clove garlic, crushed
30g/1oz plain flour
280ml/½ pint milk
1 tbsp chopped fresh parsley
1 tsp chopped fresh thyme
1 tsp tomato purée
Salt and pepper
225g/8oz fresh pasta, cooked
2 tbsps sour cream, or natural yogurt

Step 4 Stir just enough of the strained fish liquor into the sauce for it to coat the back of a spoon.

1. Cut the fish into 1-inch chunks. Put these into an ovenproof dish with the lemon juice, bay leaf, onion, peppercorns and just enough water to cover. Cover with a lid and poach for about 10 minutes in a preheated oven, 180°C/350°F/Gas Mark 4.

2. Melt the butter in a saucepan and stir in the mushrooms, pepper, shallot, paprika and garlic. Cook gently, until the pepper begins to soften.

3. Stir the flour into the mushrooms and peppers. Gradually add the milk, stirring until the sauce has thickened.

4. Remove the fish from the dish and strain off the liquor. Stir enough of this liquor into the pepper sauce to make it of coating consistency. Add the parsley, thyme and tomato purée to the sauce and simmer for 2-3 minutes. Season to taste.

5. Arrange the hot, cooked pasta on a serving plate and place the cod on top. Coat with the paprika sauce, and spoon over the sour cream, or yogurt, to serve.

Step 1 Put the cod chunks into an ovenproof dish, along with the bay leaf, lemon juice, onion slice and peppercorns. Pour in just enough water to cover the fish.

Cook's Notes

Time
Preparation takes about 20 minutes, and cooking takes about 16 minutes.

Variation
Use any other firm-fleshed whitefish, e.g. monkfish, instead of the cod.

Serving Ideas
A mixed salad would be ideal to serve with this dish.

SERVES 4

GRILLED HERRINGS WITH DILL AND MUSTARD

Dill and mustard give herring a delicious tangy flavour.

4 tbsps chopped fresh dill
6 tbsps mild Swedish mustard
2 tbsps lemon juice, or white wine
4-8 fresh herrings, cleaned but heads and tails left on
2 tbsps butter or margarine, melted
Salt and pepper

grill the fish for 5-6 minutes.

5. Turn the fish over and spread the remaining mustard and dill mixture over them. Spoon over the remaining melted butter and grill for a further 5-6 minutes.

6. Sprinkle the fish with a little salt and pepper before serving.

Step 1 In a small bowl mix the dill, mustard and lemon juice, or white wine, together thoroughly.

Step 2 Cut three slits, just piercing the skin, on both sides of each fish. Take care not to cut the fish too deeply, or the flesh may break when it is turned over.

1. Mix the dill, mustard and lemon juice, or wine, together thoroughly.

2. Cut three slits, just piercing the skin, on both sides of each herring and lay them on a grill pan.

3. Spread half the mustard mixture equally over the exposed side of each fish, pushing some into the cuts.

4. Spoon a little of the melted butter over each herring, and

Step 3 Spread half the mustard mixture equally over the top side of each fish, pushing some of the mixture gently into each cut.

Cook's Notes

Time
Preparation takes about 10 minutes, and cooking takes 12-15 minutes, although this may be longer if the herring are large.

Variation
Use whole fresh mackerel in place of the herring.

Serving Ideas
Arrange the fish on a serving dish, garnished with lemon wedges and sprigs of fresh dill. Serve with new potatoes, if available.

SERVES 4

PRAWN CRESPELLE

A delicious dish from Italy, crespelle are simply rich, wafer-thin pancakes.

3 eggs, beaten
90g/3oz plain flour
Salt
280ml/½ pint water
1 tsp olive oil
3 tbsps butter or margarine, melted
2 tbsps butter
2 tsps plain flour
420ml/¾ pint milk
Juice 1 lemon
Salt and pepper
225g/8oz prawns
Lemon slices, to garnish

1. Sift the 90g/3oz flour into a bowl, whisk the eggs into the flour gradually, until the mixture is smooth. Stir in the water and oil and leave the batter to stand for 30 minutes.

2. Heat a frying pan and brush it lightly with the melted butter. Put 1 tablespoon of the batter in the centre and roll and tilt the pan to coat the base evenly.

3. Fry until the pancake is golden brown underneath, then carefully turn over, to brown the other side. Stack and keep warm until required. Repeat until all the batter has been used up.

4. Melt the 2 tbsps of butter in a saucepan and stir in the 2 tablespoons of flour. Gradually add the milk, beating well, and returning the pan to the heat between additions, until all the milk has been incorporated. Simmer the sauce for 2-3 minutes. Stir in the lemon juice and season to taste.

5. Mix together half of the sauce and the prawns. Put one pancake into an ovenproof dish and spread a spoonful of the prawn sauce over this. Cover with another pancake and repeat the sauce/pancake procedure until all the pancakes have been used up, finishing with a pancake. Bake in a preheated oven, 190°C/375°F/Gas Mark 5, for 10 minutes.

6. Cover with the remaining sauce and garnish with lemon slices. Cut the crespelle like a cake, to serve.

Step 2 Heat and lightly grease a 7-inch frying pan. Put 1 tablespoon of batter into the centre and roll and tilt the pan, to coat the base evenly with the batter.

Step 5 Put alternate layers of pancake and sauce into an ovenproof dish. Finish with a pancake and bake.

Cook's Notes

 Time
Preparation takes about 40 minutes. Cooking takes about 30 minutes.

 Serving Ideas
Serve this dish with a colourful mixed salad.

 Freezing
Pancakes can be made in advance and frozen in stacks, with a piece of wax paper between each one To use, allow the pancakes to defrost, then reheat as required.

SERVES 4

PROVENÇALE FISH STEW

A hearty Mediterranean lunch or dinner, this dish is a real
delight for fish lovers.

1 medium onion, finely chopped
2 cloves garlic, crushed
3 tbsps olive oil
750g/1½lbs tomatoes, skinned, seeded and chopped
570ml/1 pint dry red wine
2 tbsps tomato purée
Salt and pepper
1¼ litres/2 pints fresh mussels in their shells, scrubbed
    and debearded
8 large Mediterranean prawns
120g/4oz peeled prawns
4 crab claws, shelled but with the claw tips left intact

Step 3 Cook the
mussels in the
tomato sauce,
until all the shells
have opened.

Step 1 Gently fry
the tomatoes with
the onions and
garlic, until they
are beginning to
soften.

1. In a large pan, fry the onion and garlic together gently in
the olive oil, until they are soft but not brown. Add the
tomatoes and fry until they begin to soften.

2. Stir in the red wine and the tomato purée. Season to
taste, then bring to the boil, cover and simmer for about 15
minutes.

3. Add the mussels, re-cover the pan and simmer for 5-8
minutes, or until all the mussel shells are open. Discard any
that remain closed.

4. Stir in the remaining ingredients and cook, uncovered,
for about 5-8 minutes, or until the shell fish has thoroughly
heated through.

Cook's Notes

 Time
Preparation will take about 15
minutes, plus about 10
minutes for cleaning the mussels.
Cooking takes about 35 minutes.

 Serving Ideas
Deep-fry chunks of crusty
bread, then sprinkle with garlic
salt and parsley, to serve with the fish
stew.

Preparation
To make sure the mussels are
fresh, whilst scrubbing them,
tap any open ones sharply with a knife.
If they do not shut tight, quite quickly,
discard them. Also discard any with
broken shells or that do not open after
cooking.

 Cook's Tip
If you have to keep the
mussels overnight, wrap them
in damp newspaper and store them in
the vegetable tray at the bottom of the
refrigerator.

SERVES 4

FRIED CARP

Carp is a favourite fish in Poland
and is prepared in numerous ways. This
dish is popular on Christmas Eve.

1 cleaned, filleted carp weighing about 900g-1.5kg/2-3lb
Salt
Flour
1-2 eggs, lightly beaten
Dry breadcrumbs
Butter and oil for frying

Cabbage and Mushrooms Polish Style

450g/1lb canned sauerkraut
60-90g/2-3oz dried mushrooms
30g/2 tbsps butter or margarine
1 onion, thinly sliced or finely chopped
25g/1½ tbsps flour
Salt and pepper

1. Cut the cleaned and scaled carp into even-sized portions and sprinkle lightly with salt. Leave to stand for half an hour. Skin, if desired.

2. Place the sauerkraut in a heavy-based saucepan and add 280ml/½ pint water. Bring to the boil and then allow to simmer until tender.

3. Place the mushrooms in a separate pan and add enough water to cover. Cook over gentle heat until softened. Slice the mushrooms and reserve them and their cooking liquid.

4. Melt the butter in a frying pan and, when foaming, add the onion. Cook in the butter until golden brown. Sprinkle

Step 8 Place crumbs on greaseproof paper and lift the sides to toss the crumbs over the fish.

over the flour and mix thoroughly.

5. When the sauerkraut is tender, strain the cooking liquid over the butter mixture. Stir very well and bring to the boil. Cook until thickened and add to the sauerkraut, along with the sliced mushrooms and their liquid. Stir thoroughly and set aside to keep warm.

6. Dredge the carp lightly with flour, shaking off the excess.

7. Coat with beaten egg using a pastry brush, or dip the pieces into the egg using two forks.

8. Coat the fish with the crumbs, shaking off the excess. Heat the butter and oil together in a large frying pan until very hot. Place in the fish and cook on both sides until golden brown – about 5 minutes per side. Make sure the oil and butter come half way up the sides of the fish.

9. Drain fish on paper towels and serve immediately with the cabbage and mushrooms.

Cook's Notes

Time
Sauerkraut needs about 20-25 minutes to cook until tender. Fish will take about 10 minutes for both sides. It may be necessary to cook the fish in several batches, depending on the size of frying pan.

Preparation
To make coating the fillets easier, spread the crumbs out on a sheet of greaseproof paper and place on a piece of fish coated with egg and lift the paper to toss the fillet from side to side to coat evenly.

Cook's Tip
After coating several pieces of fish, breadcrumbs may clump together with the egg. Sift the breadcrumbs through a strainer and discard the eggy bits.

SERVES 6

PAELLA

This dish has as many variations as Spain
has cooks! Fish, meat and poultry combine with
vegetables and rice to make a complete meal.

12 mussels in their shells
6 clams (if not available use 6 more mussels)
180g/6oz cod, skinned and cut into 5cm/2 inch pieces
12 Mediterranean prawns
3 chorizos or other spicy sausage
900g/2lb chicken cut in 12 serving-size pieces
1 small onion, chopped
1 clove garlic, crushed
2 small peppers, red and green, seeded and shredded
450g/1lb long grain rice
Large pinch saffron
Salt and pepper
1150ml/2 pints boiling water
120g/5oz frozen peas
3 tomatoes, peeled, seeded and chopped or shredded

1. Scrub the clams and mussels well to remove beards
and barnacles. Discard any with broken shells or those that
do not close when tapped. Leave the mussels and clams to
soak in water with a handful of flour for 30 minutes.

2. Remove the heads and legs from the prawns, if desired,
but leave on the tail shells.

3. Place the sausage in a saucepan and cover with water.
Bring to the boil and then simmer for 5 minutes. Drain and
slice into 5mm/¼ inch rounds. Set aside.

4. Heat the oil and fry the chicken pieces, browning evenly
on both sides. Remove and drain on paper towels.

5. Add the sausage, onions, garlic and peppers to the oil in
the frying pan and fry briskly for about 3 minutes.

6. Combine the sausage mixture with uncooked rice and
saffron and place in a special Paella dish or a large oven-
and flame-proof casserole. Pour on the water, season with
salt and pepper and bring to the boil. Stir occasionally and
allow to boil for about 2 minutes.

7. Add the chicken pieces and place in a preheated
200°C/400°F/Gas Mark 6 oven for about 15 minutes.

8. Add the clams, mussels, prawns, cod and peas and
cook a further 10-15 minutes or until the rice is tender,
chicken is cooked and mussels and clams open. Discard
any that do not open. Add the tomatoes 5 minutes before
the end of cooking time and serve immediately.

Step 5
Cook the saus-
ages, onions,
garlic and
peppers briefly in
oil.

Step 6
Combine the
sausage mixture,
rice and water in
a special Paella
dish or flame-
proof casserole.

Cook's Notes

 Time
Preparation takes about 30-40
minutes, cooking takes about
35-40 minutes.

 Variation
Vary the ingredients to suit
your own taste. Use other
kinds of fish and shellfish. Omit chicken
or substitute pork for part of the
quantity. Use red or spring onions if
desired and add more sausage.

 Watchpoint
Do not stir the Paella once it
goes into the oven.

SERVES 6

SINGAPORE FISH

The cuisine of Singapore was much influenced by
that of China. In turn, the Chinese brought
ingredients like curry powder into their own cuisine.

450g/1lb whitefish fillets
1 egg white
15g/1 tbsp cornflour
10ml/2 tsps white wine
Salt and pepper
Oil for frying
1 large onion, cut into 1.25cm/½ inch-thick wedges
15ml/1 tbsp mild curry powder
1 small can pineapple pieces, drained and juice
    reserved, or ½ fresh pineapple, peeled and cubed
1 small can mandarin orange segments, drained and
    juice reserved
1 small can sliced water chestnuts, drained
15g/1 tbsp cornflour mixed with juice of 1 lime
10ml/2 tsps sugar (optional)
Pinch salt and pepper

1. Starting at the tail end of the fillets, skin them using a
sharp knife.

2. Slide the knife back and forth along the length of each
fillet, pushing the fish flesh along as you go.

3. Cut the fish into even-sized pieces, about 5cm/2 inches.

4. Mix together the egg white, cornflour, wine, salt and
pepper. Place the fish in the mixture and leave to stand
while heating the oil.

5. When the oil is hot, fry a few pieces of fish at a time until
light golden brown and crisp. Remove the fish to paper
towels to drain, and continue until all the fish is cooked.

6. Remove all but 15ml/1 tbsp of the oil from the wok and
add the onion. Stir-fry the onion for 1-2 minutes and add the

curry powder. Cook the onion and curry powder for a
further 1-2 minutes. Add the juice from the pineapple and
mandarin oranges and bring to the boil.

7. Combine the cornflour and lime juice and add a
spoonful of the boiling fruit juice. Return the mixture to the
wok and cook until thickened, about 2 minutes. Taste and
add sugar if desired. Add the fruit, water chestnuts and
fried fish to the wok and stir to coat. Heat through 1 minute
and serve immediately.

Step 2 Hold
filleting knife at a
slight angle and
slide knife along
length of fillet in a
sawing motion.

Step 3 Cut fish
into even-sized
pieces, about
5cm/2 inches.

Cook's Notes

Time
Preparation takes about 25
minutes, cooking takes about
10 minutes.

Variation
Chicken may be used in place
of the fish and cooked in the
same way. Garnish with Chinese
parsley leaves if desired.

Serving Ideas
Serve with plain rice, fried rice
or cooked Chinese noodles.

SERVES 4

SKATE IN BUTTER SAUCE

This is a lovely tasting fish that
is often neglected. Once you try it,
though, you'll serve it often.

4 wings of skate
1 slice onion
2 parsley stalks
Pinch salt
6 black peppercorns

Beurre Noir

60g/4 tbsps butter
30ml/2 tbsps white wine vinegar
15ml/1 tbsp capers
15ml/1 tbsp chopped parsley (optional)

1. Place the skate in one layer in a large, deep pan. Completely cover with water and add the onion, parsley stalks, salt and peppercorns. Bring gently to the boil with pan uncovered. Allow to simmer 15-20 minutes, or until the skate is done.

2. Lift the fish out onto a serving dish and remove the skin and any large pieces of bone. Take care not to break up the fish.

3. Place the butter in a small pan and cook over high heat until it begins to brown. Add the capers and immediately remove the butter from the heat. Add the vinegar, which will cause the butter to bubble. Add parsley, if using, and pour immediately over the fish to serve.

Step 1 Place the skate in a pan with the poaching liquid and flavouring ingredients.

Step 2 Carefully remove any skin or large bones from the cooked fish, with a small knife.

Step 3 Pour sizzling butter over the fish to serve.

 *Cook's Notes*

 Variations
Chopped black olives, shallots or mushrooms may be used instead of or in addition to the capers. Add lemon juice instead of vinegar, if desired.

 Cook's Tip
When the skate is done, it will pull away from the bones in long strips.

 Time
Preparation takes about 20 minutes, cooking takes 15-20 minutes for the fish and about 5 minutes to brown the butter.

SERVES 4

FISH MILANESE

These fish, cooked in the style of
Milan, have a crispy crumb coating
and the fresh tang of lemon juice.

8 sole or plaice fillets
30ml/2 tbsps dry vermouth
1 bay leaf
90ml/6 tbsps olive oil
Salt and pepper
Seasoned flour for dredging
2 eggs, lightly beaten
Dry breadcrumbs
Oil for shallow frying
90g/6 tbsps butter
1 clove garlic, crushed
10ml/2 tsps chopped parsley
30ml/2 tbsps capers
5ml/1 tsp chopped fresh oregano
Juice of 1 lemon
Salt and pepper
Lemon wedges and parsley to garnish

1. Skin the fillets with a sharp filleting knife. Remove any small bones and place the fillets in a large, shallow dish. Combine the vermouth, oil and bay leaf in a small saucepan and heat gently. Allow to cool completely and pour over the fish. Leave the fish to marinate for about 1 hour, turning them occasionally.

2. Remove the fish from the marinade and dredge lightly with the seasoned flour.

3. Dip the fillets into the beaten eggs to coat, or use a pastry brush to brush the eggs onto the fillets. Dip the egg-coated fillet into the breadcrumbs, pressing the crumbs on firmly.

4. Heat the oil in a large frying pan. Add the fillets and cook slowly on both sides until golden brown. Cook for about 3 minutes on each side, remove and drain on paper towels.

5. Pour the oil out of the frying pan and wipe it clean. Add the butter and the garlic and cook until both turn a light brown. Add the herbs, capers and lemon juice and pour immediately over the fish. Garnish with lemon wedges and sprigs of parsley.

Step 1 Hold each fillet firmly by the tail end and work a sharp filleting knife down the length of the fillet, holding the knife at a slight angle. Keep the blade as close as possible to the fish.

Step 3 Dip or brush the fillets with the beaten egg and press on the breadcrumb coating firmly.

Cook's Notes

Time
Preparation takes 1 hour for the fish to marinate, cooking takes about 6 minutes. It may be necessary to cook the fish in several batches, depending upon the size of the frying pan.

Cook's Tip
If necessary, keep the fish fillets warm by placing on a wire cooling rack covered with paper towels and place in a warm oven, leaving the door slightly ajar. Sprinkling the fish fillets lightly with salt as they drain on paper towels helps remove some of the oil.

Variations
Other whitefish fillets may be prepared in the same way. Choose fillets that are of even size so that they cook in the same length of time. Chopped onion may be substituted for the garlic, if desired.

SERVES 4

POLISH-STYLE HERRING

Herring, prepared in any form, is a national
favourite in Poland. These fish can be prepared
well in advance and stored in their marinade.

4 even-sized herring, cleaned
2 onions, thinly sliced
10 black peppercorns
5 whole allspice berries
2 bay leaves
1 lemon, sliced
Juice of 3 lemons
140ml/¼ pint cream
2.5ml/½ tsp sugar
4 potatoes, peeled and sliced
Salt, pepper and caraway seed
90ml/6 tbsps vegetable oil
Lemon wedges and chopped parsley to garnish

1. Place fish open end downward on a chopping board.
Press along the backbone with the heel of your hand to
loosen the bone.

2. Turn over and carefully pull out the main bone.

3. Cut the fillets in half and skin them using a filleting knife,
beginning at the tail end and working up to the head end
using a sawing motion, with the knife at an angle to the skin.

4. Layer up the fillets in a deep casserole, placing onion
slices, spices, bay leaves and lemon slices between each
layer.

5. Mix lemon juice and sugar together and pour over the
fish. Place a sheet of greaseproof paper directly over the
top of the fish and cover with the casserole lid. Store in the
refrigerator for 24 hours. Remove the fillets and strain the

Step 2 Turn over
and carefully pull
out the bone.

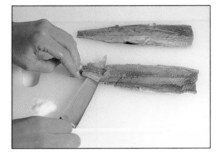

Step 3 Cut fillets
in half and skin
them using the
same knife held at
a slight angle. Dip
fingers in salt to
grip the fish skin
more easily.

liquid. Mix 60ml/4 tbsps of the liquid with the cream and
pour over the fillets to serve.

6. Layer the potatoes in an ovenproof serving dish and
sprinkle salt, pepper, and caraway seeds in between each
layer and on top. Spoon the oil over the top of the potatoes
and bake, uncovered, in a preheated 200°C/400°F/Gas
Mark 6 oven for about 30-40 minutes or until golden and
cooked through. Serve with the herring. Garnish the dish
with chopped parsley and lemon wedges.

Cook's Notes

Time
Herring takes about 25
minutes to prepare and must
marinate in the refrigerator for 24
hours. Potatoes take about 15 minutes
to prepare and 30-40 minutes to cook.

Preparation
To make the fish easier to skin,
dip fingers in salt for a better
grip on slippery skin.

Buying Guide
A fishmonger will clean and
fillet the herrings for you if
required.

SERVES 6-8

SEAFOOD TORTA

A very stylish version of a fish flan, this makes
a perfect accompaniment to an Italian aperitif or
serves as a light supper dish with salad.

Pastry

225g/8oz plain flour, sifted
120g/4oz unsalted butter
Pinch salt
60ml/4 tbsps cold milk

Filling

120g/4oz whitefish fillets (plaice, sole or cod)
225g/8oz cooked prawns
120g/4oz dressed crab
140ml/¼ pint white wine
140ml/¼ pint water
Large pinch hot pepper flakes
Salt and pepper
30g/2 tbsps butter
30g/2 tbsps flour
1 clove garlic, crushed
2 egg yolks
140ml/¼ pint double cream
Chopped fresh parsley

1. To prepare the pastry, sift the flour into a bowl or onto a work surface. Cut the butter into small pieces and begin mixing them into the flour. Mix until the mixture resembles fine breadcrumbs - this may also be done in a food processor. Make a well in the flour, pour in the milk and add the pinch of salt. Mix with a fork, gradually incorporating the butter and flour mixture from the sides until all the ingredients are mixed. This may also be done in a food processor.

2. Form the dough into a ball and knead for about 1 minute. Leave the dough in the refrigerator for about 1 hour.

3. To prepare the filling, cook whitefish fillets in the water and wine with the red pepper flakes for about 10 minutes or

Step 5 Press a sheet of grease-proof paper on the pastry and fill with beans, rice or baking beans to weight down.

until just firm to the touch. When the fish is cooked, remove it from the liquid and flake it into a bowl with the prawns and the crab meat. Reserve the cooking liquid.

4. Melt the butter in a small saucepan and stir in the flour. Gradually strain on the cooking liquid from the fish, stirring constantly until smooth. Add garlic, place over high heat and bring to the boil. Lower the heat and allow to cook for 1 minute. Add to the fish in the bowl and set aside to cool.

5. On a well-floured surface, roll out the pastry and transfer it with a rolling pin to a tart pan with a removable base. Press the dough into the pan and cut off any excess. Prick the pastry base lightly with a fork and place a sheet of greaseproof paper inside. Fill with rice, dried beans or baking beans and chill for 30 minutes. Bake the pastry shell blind for 15 minutes in a 190°C/375°F/Gas Mark 5 oven.

6. While the pastry is baking, combine the egg yolks, cream and parsley and stir into the fish filling. Adjust the seasoning with salt and pepper. When the pastry is ready, remove the paper and beans and pour in the filling.

7. Return the tart to the oven and bake for a further 25 minutes. Allow to cool slightly and then remove from the pan. Transfer to a serving dish and slice before serving.

Cook's Notes

Time
Filling takes about 15-20 minutes to prepare. Pastry takes about 20 minutes to prepare plus 1 hour refrigeration. Tart takes about 40 minutes to cook.

Variation
Substitute lobster for the whitefish for a special occasion or dinner party first course.

Freezing
Make the pastry in advance and wrap it very well. Label and freeze for up to 3 months. Defrost at room temperature before using. Also freeze uncooked in the flan dish.

SERVES 4

PLAICE AND MUSHROOM TURNOVERS

These delicious individual pies make a warming family lunch
or supper dish.

4 plaice fillets, skinned
Salt and pepper
120ml/4 fl oz milk
120g/4oz button mushrooms, trimmed and thinly sliced
2 tbsps butter
Juice 1 lemon
3 tbsps hazelnut, or lemon, stuffing mix
340g/12oz puff pastry
Beaten egg, for glazing
Poppy seeds, for sprinkling

1. Season the plaice fillets and roll them up Swiss roll fashion. Secure each roll with a cocktail stick and poach gently in the milk for about 10 minutes in a preheated oven, 180°C/350°F/Gas Mark 4.

2. Drain the fish and allow it to cool. Remove the cocktail sticks. Increase the oven temperature to 200°C/400°F/

Step 4 Allow the cooked mushrooms to cool and then stir in the stuffing mixture, making sure they are well combined.

Step 6 Pull the pastry edges up and over the fish filling. Pinch the edges together firmly to seal completely.

Gas Mark 6.

3. Put the mushrooms and butter into a pan with the lemon juice. Cook over a moderate heat for about 5 minutes.

4. Allow the mushrooms to cool and then stir in the stuffing mix.

5. Roll out the pastry, quite thinly, into 4 circles, each 6 inches in diameter. Brush the edges with beaten egg.

6. Put a fish roll into the centre of each pastry circle and top with a quarter of the mushroom mixture. Pull the pastry edges up and over the fish and pinch together to seal.

7. Place the turnovers on a greased baking sheet and glaze with the beaten egg. Sprinkle with a few poppy seeds.

8. Bake in the reset oven for about 25 minutes, or until well risen, puffed and golden. Serve piping hot.

Cook's Notes

Time
Preparation will take about 25 minutes, plus the cooling time. Cooking will take about 35 minutes.

Variation
Make these turnovers with wholemeal puff pastry for an even more nutritious dish.

Serving Ideas
Serve with new or mashed potatoes and a salad or green vegetable.

SERVES 6

SMOKED HADDOCK AND EGG QUICHE

This classic quiche is a firm favourite for lunches, buffets and suppers alike.

225g/8oz wholemeal dough
340g/12oz smoked haddock fillet
140ml/¼ pint chicken stock
2 hard-boiled eggs, chopped
1 tbsp chopped fresh chives
90g/3oz cheese, grated
3 eggs
280ml/½ pint milk
Salt and pepper

Step 1 Press the dough into a flan dish and ease a piece of wax paper over the base and against the sides of the dough case. Half fill with dried beans or peas, to bake blind.

1. Roll out the dough to fit a 9-inch deep fluted pie pan. Press the edges up well and push the base well down. Prick the base with a fork and bake blind for 15 minutes in a preheated oven, 190°C/375°F/Gas Mark 5.

2. Poach the fish gently in the chicken stock for about 8 minutes, or until just tender. Drain the fish and flake it into a bowl, discarding any skin or bones.

3. Mix the chopped eggs, chives and cheese into the fish, and spread this mixture evenly into the part-baked dough case.

4. Beat together the eggs and milk and season to taste. Pour over the fish mixture in the dough case.

5. Bake for 25-30 minutes, or until the filling is set, at the same oven temperature as before.

Step 3 Mix the chopped eggs, chives and cheese into the fish and spread this mixture evenly into the dough case.

Step 4 Carefully pour the beaten egg and milk over the fish in the dough case.

Cook's Notes

Time
Preparation will take about 25 minutes, and cooking takes about 40 minutes.

Variation
Use flaked canned tuna fish, in place of the smoked haddock.

Serving Ideas
Serve with new or jacket potatoes and a crisp salad.

SERVES 4

STEAMED FISH ROLLS

Rolled fish looks elegant and makes a dish that is slightly
out of the ordinary.

2 large sole or plaice, cut into 4 fillets
180g/6oz peeled prawns, chopped
2 tsps cornflour
1 tsp dry sherry
4 spring onions, green only, chopped
2 eggs, beaten with a pinch of salt

Step 1 Lay the fillets with the skin side down and carefully ease the meat away from the skin with a very sharp knife. Pull the skin towards you and roll the meat away, as you cut.

1. Skin the fish fillets carefully and lay them 'skin' side up on a flat surface.

2. Mix the prawn with the cornflour, sherry and onions. Divide this mixture equally between the plaice fillets.

3. Cook the eggs in a wok or frying pan, until they are softly scrambled. Spread equal quantities of this over the prawn mixture.

4. Roll up the fish fillets Swiss roll fashion, folding the thicker end over first. Secure with cocktail sticks.

5. Put the fish rolls in the top of a steamer or fish kettle and fill the bottom with boiling water. Steam for 10-15 minutes, until the fish is cooked. Remove the cocktail sticks and serve immediately.

Step 3 Cook the eggs in a wok or frying pan over a gentle heat, stirring continuously, until they are softly scrambled.

Step 4 Carefully roll up the fillets from the thickest end and secure them with a cocktail stick, while they cook.

Cook's Notes

Time
Preparation takes 25 minutes and cooking takes 10-15 minutes.

Serving Ideas
Serve with new potatoes and a fresh mixed salad.

Preparation
Whilst skinning the fillets, take care to angle the sharp blade of the knife down towards the skin, to prevent cutting the flesh.

Cook's Tip
Spread more of the filling towards the thicker end of the fillets, to help prevent it falling out as you roll.

SERVES 4

SARDINE AND TOMATO GRATINÉE

Fresh sardines are becoming more widely available and this
recipe makes the most of these delicious fish.

3 tbsps olive oil
1.2Kg/2lbs large fresh sardines, descaled and cleaned
2 leeks, cleaned and sliced
140ml/¼ pint dry white wine
225/8oz tomatoes, skinned and quartered
Salt and pepper
2 tbsps each chopped fresh basil and parsley
60g/2oz Parmesan cheese, grated
60g/2oz dry breadcrumbs

1. Heat the oil in a frying pan and fry the sardines, until they are brown on both sides. It may be necessary to do this in several batches, to prevent the fish from breaking up.

2. When all the sardines are cooked, set them aside and cook the leeks gently in the sardine oil. When the leeks are soft, pour in the wine and boil rapidly, until it is reduced by about two thirds.

3. Add the tomatoes, seasoning and herbs to the leeks and cook for about 1 minute. Pour the vegetables into an ovenproof dish and lay the sardines on top.

4. Sprinkle the cheese and breadcrumbs evenly over the sardines and bake in a preheated oven, 225°C/425°F/Gas Mark 7, for about 5 minutes.

Step 1 Fry the sardines a few at a time, to prevent them from breaking up during cooking.

Step 4 Sprinkle the Parmesan cheese and breadcrumbs evenly over the sardines, before baking them.

Cook's Notes

Time
Preparation takes about 20-25 minutes. Cooking takes about 15 minutes.

Variation
Try substituting herrings or mackerel for the sardines. They will take a little longer to fry.

Serving Ideas
Cut a few anchovy fillets in half lengthways and arrange them in a lattice on top of the gratinée, before serving with hot garlic bread.

Freezing
Sardines can be frozen for up to 2 months, but remember to clean and descale them first.

SERVES 4

COD CURRY

The fragrant spices used in this recipe are now readily available at most supermarkets.

3 tbsps vegetable oil
1 large onion, peeled and chopped
2.5cm/1-inch piece cinnamon stick
1 bay leaf
1 tsp ginger paste
1 tsp garlic paste
1 tsp chilli powder
1 tsp ground cumin
1 tsp ground coriander
¼ tsp ground turmeric
140ml/¼ pint natural yogurt OR
225g/8oz can tomatoes, chopped
1-2 fresh green chillies, chopped
2 sprigs fresh coriander leaves, chopped
1 tsp salt
1lb cod cutlets, or fillets, cut into 2-inch pieces

1. In a large heavy-based saucepan, fry the onion in the oil until golden brown. Add the cinnamon, bay leaf and the ginger and garlic pastes and fry for 1 minute.

2. Add the ground spices and fry for a further minute, then stir in *either* the yogurt, *or* the canned tomatoes and the chopped chillies and coriander leaves.

3. Only if you have used yogurt, stir in 140ml/¼ pint water

Step 1 Fry the cinnamon, bay leaf and the ginger and garlic pastes with the onions for 1 minute.

Step 4 Add the cod pieces to the sauce in the pan, stir well to coat thoroughly, before covering and simmering for 15-18 minutes.

and simmer the mixture for 2-3 minutes. Do not add any water if you have used the canned tomatoes.

4. Stir the cod into the sauce, and add the salt. Cover the pan and simmer for 15-18 minutes before serving.

Cook's Notes

Time
Preparation takes about 15 minutes, and cooking takes about 20 minutes.

Cook's Tip
Great care should be taken when preparing fresh chillies. Always wash hands thoroughly afterwards, and avoid getting any juice in the eyes or mouth. Rinse with copious amounts of clear water if this happens. For a milder curry, remove the seeds; for a hotter curry, leave them in.

Serving Ideas
Serve with boiled rice and a cucumber raita.

SERVES 6

PRAWNS AND GINGER

Quick and easy to prepare, this dish is really delicious and
also very nutritious.

2 tbsps oil
675g/1½lbs peeled prawns
1-inch piece fresh root ginger, peeled and finely chopped
2 cloves of garlic, peeled and finely chopped
2-3 spring onions, chopped
1 leek, white part only, cut into strips
120g/4oz peas, shelled
180g/6oz bean sprouts
2 tbsps dark soy sauce
1 tsp sugar
Pinch salt

1. Heat the oil in a wok and stir-fry the prawns for 2-3 minutes. Set the prawns aside.

2. Reheat the oil and add the ginger and garlic. Stir quickly, then add the onions, leek and peas. Stir-fry for 2-3 minutes.

3. Add the bean sprouts and prawns to the cooked vegetables. Stir in the soy sauce, sugar and salt and cook for 2 minutes. Serve immediately.

Step 2 Stir-fry the onions, leek and peas for 2-3 minutes.

Step 3 Cook all the ingredients together for 2 minutes before serving.

Cook's Notes

Time
Preparation takes about 10 minutes, and cooking takes about 7-9 minutes.

Preparation
The vegetables can be prepared in advance and kept in airtight plastic boxes in the refrigerator for up to 6 hours before needed.

Serving Ideas
Serve this on its own with rice or pasta, or as part of an authentic Chinese meal.

SERVES 4
TROUT WITH HERBS

The miller (meunier) caught trout fresh from the mill stream and his wife used the flour which was on hand to dredge them with, or so the story goes.

4 even-sized trout, cleaned and trimmed
Flour
Salt and pepper
120g/4oz butter
Juice of 1 lemon
30ml/2 tbsps chopped fresh herbs such as parsley,
    chervil, tarragon, thyme or marjoram
Lemon wedges to garnish

1. Trim the trout tails to make them more pointed. Rinse the trout well.

2. Dredge the trout with flour and shake off the excess. Season with salt and pepper. Heat half the butter in a very large sauté pan and, when foaming, place in the trout. It may be necessary to cook the trout in two batches to avoid overcrowding the pan.

3. Cook over fairly high heat on both sides to brown evenly. Depending on size, the trout should take 5-8 minutes per side to cook. The dorsal fin will pull out easily when the trout are cooked. Remove the trout to a serving dish and keep them warm.

4. Wipe out the pan and add the remaining butter. Cook over moderate heat until beginning to brown, then add the lemon juice and herbs. When the lemon juice is added, the butter will bubble up and sizzle. Pour immediately over the fish and serve with lemon wedges.

Step 1 Trim the trout tails with scissors to make them neater.

Step 2 Coat trout in flour, shaking off excess.

Step 3 Brown the trout on both sides. Dorsal fin will pull out easily when done.

Cook's Notes

Time
Preparation takes 15-20 minutes, cooking takes 5-8 minutes per side for the fish and about 5 minutes to brown the butter.

Preparation
If trout is coated in flour too soon before cooking it will become soggy.

Serving Ideas
Serve with new potatoes and peeled, cubed cucumber quickly sautéed in butter and chopped dill.

SERVES 6

PRAWN EGG RICE

Serve this on its own for a tasty lunch or supper dish, or as part of a more elaborate Chinese meal.

450g/1lb long grain rice
2 eggs
½ tsp salt
4 tbsps oil
2 spring onions, chopped
1 large onion, chopped
2 cloves of garlic, chopped
120g/4oz peeled prawns
60g/2oz shelled peas
2 tbsps dark soy sauce

Step 4 Cook the eggs with the onions gently, until set and softly scrambled.

Step 3 Rinse the rice in cold water and separate the grains with a fork.

1. Wash the rice thoroughly and put it in a saucepan. Add water to come 1 inch above the top of the rice.

2. Bring the rice to the boil, stir once, then reduce the heat.

Cover and simmer the rice for 5-7 minutes, or until the liquid has been absorbed.

3. Rinse the rice in cold water and fluff up with a fork, to separate the grains.

4. Beat the eggs with a pinch of salt. Heat 1 tablespoon of the oil in a wok and cook the onions until soft, but not brown. Pour in the egg and stir gently, until the mixture is set. Remove the egg mixture and set it aside.

5. Heat a further tablespoon of the oil and fry the garlic, prawns, peas and spring onions quickly for 2 minutes. Remove from the wok and set aside.

6. Heat the remaining oil in the wok and stir in the rice and remaining salt. Stir-fry, to heat the rice through, then add the egg and the prawn mixtures and the soy sauce, stirring to blend thoroughly. Serve immediately.

Cook's Notes

Time
Preparation takes about 20 minutes and cooking takes about 15 minutes.

Variation
Use chopped red peppers or corn kernels, instead of the peas.

Freezing
Rice can be cooked and frozen for up to 6 weeks. Frozen rice should be defrosted and rinsed, before being used in this dish.

SERVES 4

BAKED STUFFED MACKEREL

Mackerel should be eaten the day it is caught, so this is a
recipe for people living near the sea.

60g/2oz polyunsaturated margarine
1 small onion, finely chopped
1 tbsp medium oatmeal
60g/2oz fresh wholemeal breadcrumbs
1 1/2 tsps chopped fresh lemon thyme
1 1/2 tsps chopped fresh parsley
Freshly ground sea salt and black pepper
2-3 tbsps hot water, if required
4 mackerel, cleaned and washed thoroughly

Step 1 Fry the chopped onion, until it is soft but not coloured.

1. In a large frying pan, melt the margarine. Fry the chopped onion in the margarine until it is soft, but not coloured.

2. Add the oatmeal, breadcrumbs, herbs and seasoning to the fried onion, and mix well to form a firm stuffing, adding a little hot water to bind, if necessary.

3. Fill the cavities of the fish with the stuffing and wrap each one separately in well-greased aluminium foil.

4. Place each fish parcel in a roasting pan, or on a baking sheet, and cook in a preheated oven, 190°C/375°F/Gas Mark 5, for half an hour.

Step 2 Add the oatmeal, breadcrumbs, herbs and seasoning to the fried onion, and mix well to form a firm stuffing, binding with a little of the hot water, if necessary.

Step 3 Fill the cavities of each fish with equal amounts of the onion and oatmeal stuffing. Push the stuffing well into the back of the fish to preserve its shape.

Cook's Notes

Time
Preparation takes about 15 minutes, and cooking takes about 30 minutes.

Variation
The stuffing in this recipe is also delicious with herrings, or whiting.

Serving Ideas
Serve this dish garnished with fresh watercress and new potatoes.

SERVES 4
COCONUT FRIED FISH WITH CHILLIES

A real treat for lovers of spicy food.

Oil for frying
450g/1lb sole or plaice fillets, skinned, boned and cut
   into 2.5cm/1-inch strips
Seasoned flour
1 egg, beaten
60g/2oz desiccated coconut
1 tbsp vegetable oil
1 tsp grated fresh ginger
¼ tsp chilli powder
1 red chilli, seeded and finely chopped
1 tsp ground coriander
½ tsp ground nutmeg
1 clove garlic, crushed
2 tbsps tomato purée
2 tbsps tomato chutney
2 tbsps dark soy sauce
2 tbsps lemon juice
2 tbsps water
1 tsp brown sugar
Salt and pepper

Step 1 Toss the strips of fish in the flour and then dip them in the beaten egg. Roll them finally in the desiccated coconut. Do not coat the fish too soon before frying.

Step 2 Fry the fish in the hot oil, a few pieces at a time, to prevent it from breaking up.

1. In a frying pan, heat about 2 inches of oil to 190°C/375°F. Toss the fish strips in the seasoned flour and then dip them into the beaten egg. Roll them in the desiccated coconut and shake off the excess.

2. Fry the fish, a few pieces at a time, in the hot oil and drain them on paper towels. Keep warm.

3. Heat the 1 tbsp oil in a wok or frying pan and fry the ginger, red chilli, spices and garlic, for about 2 minutes.

4. Add the remaining ingredients and simmer for about 3 minutes. Serve the fish, with the sauce handed round separately.

Cook's Notes

Time
Preparation takes about 30 minutes, and cooking takes about 30 minutes.

Cook's Tip
Great care should be taken when preparing fresh chillies. Always wash your hands thoroughly afterwards, and avoid getting any juice in your eyes or mouth. Rinse with copious amounts of clear water, if you do.

Variation
Substitute a firm fleshed fish like haddock, or monkfish, for the plaice.

Serving Ideas
Serve with plain boiled rice, a cucumber relish and plenty of salad.

Chapter IV

DISHES WITH A DIFFERENCE

SERVES 4

TUNA BAKED IN PARCHMENT

This recipe uses a French technique that is
healthy and seals in all the flavour too.

4 tuna steaks, about 8oz each in weight
1 red onion, thinly sliced
1 beefsteak tomato, cut in 4 slices
1 green pepper, seeded and cut in thin rings
8 large, uncooked peeled prawns
2 tsps finely chopped fresh oregano
1 small green or red chilli, seeded and finely chopped
60ml/4 tbsps dry white wine or lemon juice
Salt
Oil

Step 1-4 Layer the ingredients on oiled parchment.

1. Lightly oil 4 oval pieces of baking parchment about 8 × 10 ".

2. Place a tuna steak on half of each piece of parchment and top with 2 slices of onion.

3. Place a slice of tomato on each fish and top with green pepper rings.

4. Place 2 prawns on top and sprinkle over the oregano,

salt and chilli pepper.

5. Spoon the wine or lemon juice over each fish and fold the parchment over the fish.

6. Overlap the edges and pinch and fold to seal securely. Place the parcels on a baking sheet.

7. Bake for about 10-12 minutes in a pre-heated 200°C/400°F/Gas Mark 6 oven.

8. Unwrap each parcel at the table to serve.

Step 6 Overlap the edges of the parchment, but don't enclose fish too tightly.

Step 6 Use thumb and forefinger to pinch and fold the overlapped edge to seal.

Cook's Notes

Time
Preparation takes about 35 minutes and cooking takes about 10-12 minutes.

Preparation
The dish may be prepared up to 6 hours in advance and kept in the refrigerator. Remove about 30 minutes before cooking and allow fish to come to room temperature.

Variation
Other fish, such as swordfish or halibut, can be used in place of the tuna. Any thinly-sliced vegetable other than potato can be used.

SERVES 4

SCAMPI AURORA

The name comes from the rosy pink
sauce. For the occasional extravagant
dinner, this dish is perfect!

90g/6 tbsps butter or margarine
1 small onion, chopped
450g/1lb scampi
90g/6 tbsps flour
280ml/½ pint water or fish stock
15ml/1 tbsp tomato purée
30ml/2 tbsps chopped parsley
10ml/2 tsps chopped dill
Salt and pepper
Cooked rice

brown, stirring frequently.

3. Pour on the water and stir vigorously to blend. Add tomato purée and bring to the boil. Add parsley, dill, and seasoning to taste and return the onions and the scampi to the sauce. Heat through for 5 minutes and serve over rice.

Step 3 Add the water gradually, stirring vigorously. The mixture should be very thick.

Step 1 Cook the onion and scampi quickly until the scampi curls up.

Step 3 Return the scampi and onions to the sauce to heat through. Juices from both will thin down the sauce.

1. Melt half the butter or margarine, add the onion and cook to soften slightly. Add scampi and cook quickly until it curls. Remove to a plate.

2. Add the flour to the pan and cook slowly until golden

Cook's Notes

Time
Preparation takes about 20 minutes and cooking takes about 15 minutes.

Watchpoint
Prawns, scampi and other types of seafood become very tough if cooked too quickly or over heat that is too high.

Variation
Scampi are usually available from fishmongers. If you can't get them use cooked, peeled prawns. Add them at the last and heat through 5 minutes.

SERVES 4

SALMON PIES

Use economical canned pink
salmon in a very unusual
and tasty way.

Pastry
225g/8oz plain flour, sifted
Pinch salt
120-180g/4-6oz butter or margarine
Cold water

Filling
1 large can pink salmon
45ml/3 tbsps oil
45g/3 tbsps flour
½ green pepper, seeded and finely diced
2 spring onions, finely chopped
1 stick celery, finely chopped
280ml/½ pint
Salt and pepper

Step 6 Roll the pastry out thinly and use a rolling pin to transfer it to the baking dish.

1. Sift the flour in a bowl with a pinch of salt and rub in the butter or margarine until the mixture resembles the breadcrumbs. Add enough cold water to bring the mixture together. Knead into a ball, wrap well and chill for about 30 minutes before use.

2. Drain salmon and remove any skin. Discard small bones.

3. Heat the oil in a small saucepan for the filling and add the flour. Cook slowly, stirring constantly until the flour turns a rich dark brown.

4. Add the remaining filling ingredients, stirring constantly while adding the milk. Bring to the boil, reduce the heat and cook for about 5 minutes. Add the salmon to the sauce.

5. Divide the pastry into 4 and roll out each portion on a lightly-floured surface to about 5mm/¼ inch thick.

6. Line individual flan or pie dishes with the pastry, pushing it carefully onto the base and down the sides, taking care not to stretch it. Trim off excess pastry and reserve.

7. Place a sheet of greaseproof paper or foil on the pastry and pour on rice, pasta or baking beans to come halfway up the sides. Bake the pastry blind for about 10 minutes in a pre-heated 200°C/400°F/Gas Mark 6 oven.

8. Remove the paper and beans and bake for an additional 5 minutes to cook the base.

9. Spoon in the filling and roll out any trimmings to make a lattice pattern on top. Bake a further 10 minutes to brown the lattice and heat the filling. Cool slightly before serving.

Cook's Notes

Time
Preparation takes about 30 minutes and cooking takes about 10 minutes for the filling and 25 minutes to finish the dish.

Cook's Tip
Baking the pastry blind helps it to crisp on the base and brown evenly without overcooking the filling.

Serving Ideas
Serve as a light main course with a salad, or make smaller pies to serve as a first course.

SERVES 4
PRAWN PROVENÇALE

Deceptively simple, this dish combines all
the ingredients that are easy to find and
that almost everyone enjoys.

60ml/4 tbsps oil
2 large green peppers, seeded and cut into 2.5cm/1
  inch pieces
3 sticks celery, sliced
2 medium onions, diced
2 cloves garlic, crushed
2 400g/14oz cans tomatoes
2 bay leaves
Pinch salt and pepper
Pinch thyme
30g/2 tbsps cornflour mixed with 45ml/3 tbsps dry white
  wine
450g/1lb cooked, peeled prawns

1. Place the oil in a large saucepan and add the vegetables. Cook for a few minutes over gentle heat and add the garlic.

2. Add the tomatoes and their juice, breaking up the tomatoes with a fork or a potato masher. Add the bay leaves, cayenne pepper or tabasco, seasoning and thyme, and bring to the boil. Allow to simmer for about 5 minutes, uncovered.

3. Mix a few spoonfuls of the hot tomato liquid with the cornflour mixture and then return it to the saucepan. Bring to the boil, stirring constantly until thickened.

4. Simmer over gentle heat for about 15 minutes. Add the prawns and heat through gently for 5 minutes.

5. Remove the bay leaves before serving, and spoon the sauce over rice.

Step 1 Cook the vegetables and garlic briefly in hot oil to soften slightly.

Step 3 Mix a few spoonfuls of the hot tomato liquid into the cornflour mixture and then return to the saucepan.

Step 4 Add prawns to the tomato sauce and cook until they curl up and turn pink.

Cook's Notes

Time
Preparation takes about 25 minutes and cooking takes about 20-30 minutes. Rice will take about 10-12 minutes to boil.

Cook's Tip
Do not allow prawns or other shellfish to cook too rapidly or for too long, as this will toughen them.

Variation
An equal amount of cooked white fish or even boned and cooked chicken can be substituted for the prawns.

SERVES 6

SPICY SEAFOOD MIX

This dish is a relative of American gumbos –
rich, spicy stews full of flavour.

450g/1lb cooked, unpeeled prawns
½ tbsp each whole cloves, whole allspice, coriander
   seed and mustard seed
1150ml/2 pints water
60g/4 tbsps butter or margarine
1 onion, peeled and sliced
1 green pepper, seeded and sliced
2 cloves garlic, finely chopped
45g/3 tbsps flour
½ tsp thyme
1 bay leaf
2 tbsps chopped parsley
Dash Worcester sauce
12 oysters, shelled
225g/8oz tomatoes, peeled and chopped
Salt and pepper
Cooked rice

Step 1 Peel the prawns, adding the heads, tail shell, legs and roe, if present, to the spice mixture in a large stock pot.

1. Peel the prawns and reserve the shells. Mix shells with the spice mixture and water and bring to the boil in a large stock pot. Reduce the heat and allow to simmer for about 20 minutes.

2. Melt the butter or margarine and, when foaming, add the onion, green pepper, garlic and flour. Cook slowly, stirring constantly until the flour is a pale golden brown. Gradually strain on the stock, discarding the shells and spice mixture. Add the thyme and bay leaf and stir well. Bring to the boil and then simmer until thick.

Step 3 Loosen the oysters from their shells and add to the hot mix. If desired, strain the oyster liquid through a very fine mesh strainer.

3. Add the parsley and the Worcester sauce to taste. Add the oysters, peeled prawns and tomatoes and heat through gently to cook the oysters.

4. Adjust the seasoning and serve over rice.

Cook's Notes

Time
Preparation takes about 25-30 minutes and cooking takes about 20-25 minutes.

Variation
If they are available, use raw, unpeeled prawns and cook with the water and the spice mixture until they turn pink and curl up. Drain them, reserving the liquid. Peel and return the shells to the stock. Re-boil the stock and allow to simmer for about 15 minutes.

Cook's Tip
If the mixture is not thick enough, use equal portions of butter or margarine and flour mixed together to a paste. Add a bit of the paste at a time to the mix, and boil in between additions until the desired thickness is reached.

SERVES 4-6

PRAWN RISOTTO

An easy and extremely satisfying dish of rice and seafood.
Sometimes garlic sausage is added for extra spice.

30g/2 tbsps butter or margarine
30g/2 tbsps flour
1 medium onion, finely chopped
1 clove garlic, crushed
1 red pepper, seeded and finely chopped
400g/14oz canned tomatoes
1150ml/2 pints fish or chicken stock
¼ tsp ground ginger
Pinch allspice
1 tsp chopped fresh thyme or ½ tsp dried thyme
¼ tsp cayenne pepper
Pinch salt
Dash Tabasco
100g/4oz uncooked rice
900g/2lbs uncooked prawns, peeled
2 spring onions, chopped to garnish

1. Melt the butter in a heavy-based saucepan and then add the flour. Stir to blend well and cook over low heat until a pale straw colour. Add the onion, garlic and pepper and cook until soft.

2. Add the tomatoes and their juice, breaking up the tomatoes with a fork or a potato masher. Add the stock and mix well. Add the ginger, allspice, thyme, cayenne pepper, salt and Tabasco. Bring to the boil and allow to boil rapidly, stirring for about 2 minutes.

3. Add the rice, stir well and cover the pan. Cook for about 15-20 minutes, or until the rice is tender and has absorbed most of the liquid.

4. Add the prawns during the last 10 minutes of cooking time. Cook until the prawns curl and turn pink. Adjust the seasoning, spoon into a serving dish and sprinkle with the chopped spring onion to serve.

Step 1 Cook the flour and butter roux until it is a pale straw colour.

Step 3 Add the uncooked rice directly into the sauce and stir well.

Cook's Notes

Time
Preparation takes about 40 minutes and cooking takes about 25-30 minutes.

Cook's Tip
If the rice still has a lot of liquid left before adding the prawn, uncover and boil rapidly, stirring once or twice, for about 5 minutes. This should evaporate excess liquid.

Variation
If desired, use fresh tomatoes, peeled, seeded and chopped. Add about 3 fl oz extra stock. Green pepper may be used instead of red pepper, if desired.

PRAWN AND SCALLOP STIR-FRY

Pine nuts and spinach give an unusual
twist to this delicious dish.

45ml/3 tbsps oil
60g/4 tbsps pine nuts
450g/1lb uncooked prawns
450g/1lb shelled scallops, quartered if large
2 tsps grated fresh ginger
1 small red or green chilli, seeded and finely chopped
2 cloves garlic, finely chopped
1 large red pepper, seeded and cut into 2.5cm/1"
    diagonal pieces
225g/8oz fresh spinach, stalks removed and leaves well
    washed and shredded
4 spring onions, cut in 1.5cm/½" diagonal pieces
60ml/4 tbsps fish or chicken stock
60ml/4 tbsps light soy sauce
60ml/4 tbsps rice wine or dry sherry
1 tbsp cornflour

1. Heat oil in a wok and add the pine nuts. Cook over low heat, stirring continuously until lightly browned. Remove with a draining spoon and drain on paper towels.

2. Add the prawns and scallops to the oil remaining in the wok and stir over moderate heat until shellfish is beginning to look opaque and firm and the prawns look pink.

3. Add the ginger, chilli, garlic and red pepper and cook a few minutes over moderately high heat.

4. Add the spinach and onion, and stir-fry briefly. Mix the remaining ingredients together and pour over the ingredients in the wok.

5. Turn up the heat to bring the liquid to the boil, stirring ingredients constantly. Once the liquid thickens and clears, stir in the pine nuts and serve immediately.

Step 1 Cook pine nuts in oil until they are light brown.

Step 2 Cook shellfish until prawns begin to turn pink and scallops lose their transparency.

Step 5 When all ingredients are added, cook briskly to thicken the sauce.

Cook's Notes

Time
Preparation takes about 35 minutes, cooking takes about 8-10 minutes.

Preparation
Because cooking time is so short, be sure to prepare all ingredients and have them ready before beginning to stir-fry.

Economy
Eliminate scallops and cut the quantity of prawns in half. Make up the difference with a firm whitefish cut into 2.5cm/1" pieces.

SERVES 4-6

SHELLFISH BOIL

Chilli peppers add a tangy flavour
to this tasty mixture.

6 pints water
1 lemon, quartered
1 onion, cut in half but not peeled
1 celery stick, cut in 3 pieces
2 cloves garlic, left whole
Pinch salt
4 bay leaves, finely crumbled
4 dried red chilli peppers, crumbled
1 tbsp each whole cloves, whole allspice, coriander
    seed and mustard seed
1 tbsp dill weed, fresh or dry
2 tsps celery seed
450g/1lb raw, unpeeled prawns
900g/2lbs mussels, well scrubbed

Step 3 Remove the seaweed beards and any barnacles from the mussel shells.

Step 2 Add the prawns to the boiling liquid and cook them until pink and curled.

1. Place the water, lemon, onion, celery, garlic, salt, bay leaves and spices together in a large pot and cover. Bring to the boil, reduce the heat and cook slowly for 20 minutes.

2. Add the prawns in two batches and cook until pink and curled. Remove with a draining spoon.

3. Remove the seaweed beards from the mussels, and discard any that do not close when tapped.

4. Add mussels to the pot and cook, stirring frequently, for about 5 minutes or until shells have opened. Discard any that do not open.

5. Spoon prawns and mussels into serving bowls and serve immediately.

Cook's Notes

Time
Preparation takes about 30 minutes, cooking takes about 20 minutes to boil the stock and about 5 minutes for each batch of prawns and mussels.

Serving Ideas
Serve as a starter, or double the quantity for a main course.

Variation
Crabs can also be used in this dish.

SERVES 4

SPICY FRIED FISH

The spice mixture is *very* hot,
so use less if you want.

4 fish fillets, about 225g/8oz each
225g/8oz unsalted butter
15ml/1 tbsp paprika
5ml/1 tsp garlic granules
5ml/1 tsp cayenne pepper
2.5ml/½ tsp ground white pepper
10ml/2 tsps salt
5ml/1 tsp dried thyme

Step 2 Use a pastry brush to coat the fish well on both sides with the melted butter. Alternatively, spoon the butter over or dip the fish in the butter.

1. Melt the butter and pour about half into each of four ramekin dishes and set aside.

2. Brush each fish fillet liberally with the remaining butter on both sides.

3. Mix together the spices and thyme and sprinkle generously on each side of the fillets, patting it on by hand.

4. Heat a large frying pan and add about 15ml/1 tbsp butter per fish fillet. When the butter is hot, add the fish, skin side down first.

5. Turn the fish over when the underside is very brown and repeat with the remaining side. Add more butter as necessary during cooking.

6. When the top side of the fish is very dark brown, repeat with the remaining fish fillets, keeping them warm while cooking the rest.

7. Serve the fish immediately with the dishes of butter for dipping.

Step 3 Mix the seasoning ingredients together well and press firmly onto both sides of the fish to coat.

Step 5 Cook the underside and topside of the fish until very dark brown.

Cook's Notes

Time
Preparation takes about 20 minutes and cooking takes about 2 minutes per side for each fillet.

Variation
Use whatever varieties of fish fillets or steaks you like but make sure they are approximately 2cm ¾ inch thick.

Preparation
The fish should be very dark brown on the top and the bottom before serving. Leave at least 2 minutes before attempting to turn the fish over.

SERVES 4

BOILED LOBSTER

A whole lobster is sure to impress
and if you can only afford one,
share it out as a starter.

4 1lb lobsters
Water
Salt or seaweed
250ml/9fl oz melted butter
Lemon wedges
Parsley sprigs

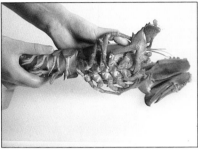

Separate body from tail by arching the lobster backwards. Break off the flipper and push the tail meat out with a fork.

Once the claws are removed from the lobster by twisting off, crack each claw with a nutcracker, hammer or special lobster cracking tool.

Remove the back from the body and discard the stomach sac and lungs. Retain the tomalley or liver to eat, if desired, and crack open the body to extract any remaining meat.

1. Fill a large stock pot full of water and add salt or a piece of seaweed. Bring the water to the boil and then turn off the heat.

2. Place the live lobsters into the pot, keeping your hand well away from the claws. Lower them in claws first.

3. Bring the water slowly back to the boil and cook the lobsters for about 15 minutes, or until they turn bright red.

4. Remove them from the water and drain briefly on paper towels. Place on a plate and garnish the plate with lemon wedges and parsley sprigs. Serve with individual dishes of melted butter for dipping. To extract meat see above.

Cook's Notes

Time
Allow about 20 minutes for the water to boil, and 15 minutes for cooking the lobster.

Preparation
This method of cooking puts the lobster gently to sleep and makes the lobster flesh much more tender. Claws can be partially cracked before serving, if desired.

Cook's Tip
Lobster may be cooked in this way for a variety of recipes that are based on pre-cooked lobster.

SERVES 4

CRUNCHY COD

Cod provides the perfect base for a
crunchy, slightly spicy topping.

4 even-sized cod fillets
Salt and pepper
90g/6 tbsps butter, melted
90g/3oz dry breadcrumbs
5ml/1 tsp dry mustard
5ml/1 tsp minced onion
Dash Worcester sauce and tabasco
30ml/2 tbsps lemon juice
15ml/1 tbsp finely chopped parsley

Step 3 Press the crumbs gently to pack them into place using a spoon or your hand.

Step 1 Season the fish lightly with salt and pepper and brush with some of the melted butter. Grill to pre-cook but do not brown.

1. Season the fish fillets with salt and pepper and place them on a grill tray. Brush with butter and grill for about 5 minutes.

2. Combine remaining butter with breadcrumbs, mustard, onion salt, Worcester sauce, tabasco, lemon juice and parsley.

3. Spoon the mixture carefully on top of each fish fillet, covering it completely. Press down lightly to pack the crumbs into place. Grill for a further 5-7 minutes, or until the top is lightly browned and the fish flakes.

Cook's Notes

Time
Preparation takes about 15 minutes and cooking takes about 12 minutes.

Preparation
If desired, the fish may also be baked in the oven. Cover the fish with foil foe first 5 minutes of baking time, uncover and top with the breadcrumb mixture. Bake for a further 10-12 minutes at 180°C/350°F/Gas Mark 4.

Variation
The breadcrumb topping may be used on other fish such as haddock, halibut or sole.

SERVES 4

STUFFED BAKED TROUT

Three kinds of ground pepper make this
stuffing quite spicy. Cut down the
amount a bit, if liked.

4 whole trout, about 225g/8oz each
120g/4oz butter or margarine
1 onion, finely chopped
2 sticks celery, finely chopped
1 small red pepper, seeded and finely chopped
4 spring onions, finely chopped
1 clove garlic, crushed
10ml/2 tsps chopped parsley
5ml/1 tsp chopped fresh dill
1.25ml/¼ tsp white pepper
1.25ml/¼ tsp cayenne pepper
1.25ml/¼ tsp black pepper
Pinch salt
120g/4oz dry breadcrumbs
2 small eggs, lightly beaten

Step 1 Trim the
fins, neaten the
tail of the trout and
rinse well. Pat dry.

Step 5 Spoon
some of the
stuffing into the
cavity of each fish.

1. Wash the trout well inside and pat dry.

2. Melt half the butter or margarine in a medium saucepan. Add onions, celery, red pepper, spring onions and
garlic. Cook over a moderate heat for about 3 minutes to
soften the vegetables. Stir in the white pepper, cayenne
pepper and black pepper, dill and parsley.

3. Remove from the heat, add the breadcrumbs and
gradually beat in the egg, adding just enough to hold the
stuffing ingredients together. Season with salt.

4. Stuff the cavity of each trout with an equal amount of the
stuffing and place the trout in a baking dish.

5. Spoon over the remaining butter and bake, uncovered,
in a pre-heated 180°C/350°F/Gas Mark 4 oven for about 25
minutes. Brown under a pre-heated grill before serving, if
desired.

Cook's Notes

Time
Preparation takes about 30
minutes and cooking takes
about 30 minutes.

Variation
Other varieties of fish, such as
sea bass or grey mullet can
also be used.

£ Economy
Since oysters are expensive,
they may be omitted from the
recipe or may be replaced with
mussels, if desired. Canned oysters,
which are somewhat cheaper, may also
be used.

SERVES 4

SNAPPER WITH FENNEL AND ORANGE SALAD

This makes a lovely summer meal. Substitute another
kind of fish if you can't get snapper.

Oil
4 even-sized red snapper, cleaned, heads and tails on
2 heads fennel
2 oranges
Juice of 1 lemon
45ml/3 tbsps light salad oil
Pinch sugar, salt and black pepper

Step 1 Make three cuts in the side of each fish for even cooking.

1. Brush both sides of the fish with oil and cut three slits in the sides of each. Sprinkle with a little of the lemon juice, reserving the rest.

2. Slice the fennel in half and remove the cores. Slice thinly. Also slice the green tops and chop the feathery herb to use in the dressing.

3. Peel the oranges, removing all the white pith.

4. Cut the oranges into segments. Peel and segment over a bowl to catch the juice.

5. Add lemon juice to any orange juice collected in the bowl. Add the oil, salt, pepper and a pinch of sugar, if necessary. Mix well and add the fennel, green herb tops and orange segments, stirring carefully. Grill the fish 3-5 minutes per side, depending on thickness. Serve the fish with the heads and tails on, accompanied by the salad.

Step 2 Slice the fennel in half and remove the cores.

Step 4 Peel and segment the oranges over a bowl to catch the juice.

Cook's Notes

Time
Preparation takes about 30 minutes and cooking takes about 6-10 minutes.

Variation
Substitute red mullet or any of the exotic fish from the Seychelles. Whole trout can also be used.

Cook's Tip
When grilling whole fish, making several cuts on the side of each fish will help to cook it quickly and evenly throughout.

SERVES 6-8

CALIFORNIAN FISH STEW

This famous and delicious fish
stew is Italian in heritage; but a close
relative of French Bouillabaisse, too.

450g/1lb spinach, well washed
1 tbsp each chopped fresh basil, thyme, rosemary and
   sage
30g/2 tbsps chopped fresh marjoram
60g/4 tbsps chopped parsley
1 large red pepper, seeded and finely chopped
2 cloves garlic, crushed
24 large fresh clams or 48 mussels, well scrubbed
1 large crab, cracked
450g/1lb monkfish or rock salmon
12 large prawns, cooked and unpeeled
450g/1lb canned plum tomatoes and juice
2 tbsps tomato purée
60ml/4 tbsps olive oil
Pinch salt and pepper
125ml–250ml dry white wine
Water

1. Chop the spinach leaves roughly after removing any
tough stems.

2. Combine the spinach with the herbs, chopped red
pepper and garlic, and set aside.

3. Discard any clams or mussels with broken shells or
ones that do not close when tapped. Place the shellfish in
the bottom of a large pot and sprinkle over a layer of the
spinach mixture.

4. Prepare the crab as for Dressed Crab Salad, leaving
the shells on the claws after cracking them slightly. Place
the crab on top of the spinach and then add another
spinach layer.

5. Add the fish and a spinach layer, followed by the
prawns and any remaining spinach.

6. Mix the tomatoes, tomato purée, oil, wine and
seasonings and pour over the seafood and spinach.

7. Cover the pot and simmer the mixture for about 40
minutes. If more liquid is necessary, add water. Spoon into
soup bowls, dividing the fish and shell fish evenly.

Step 3 Place well
scrubbed clams
or mussels in the
bottom of a large
pot, sprinkling
over spinach
mixture.

Step 6 Pour the
tomato purée and
wine mixture over
the layered
seafood and
spinach.

Cook's Notes

Time
Preparation takes about 40
minutes and cooking takes
about 40 mintues.

Preparation
Soup must be eaten
immediately after cooking. It
does not keep or reheat well.

Variation
The choice of seafood or fish
may be changed to suit your
own taste and budget. For special
occasions, add lobster.

SERVES 4

WHOLE BAKED STUFFED FISH

Biscuit crumbs add an unusual texture
to the stuffing in this tasty dish.

2kg/4¼lb whole fish, gutted and boned (use salmon,
    salmon trout or sea bass)

Stuffing
225g/8oz savoury biscuit crumbs
60g/4 tbsps butter, melted
Pinch salt and pepper
10ml/2 tsps lemon juice
1.25ml/¼ tsp each dried thyme, sage and marjoram
1 shallot, finely chopped
120g/4oz button mushrooms, chopped

Step 3 Spoon the stuffing into the cavity of the fish.

Step 2 Place the prepared fish on lightly-greased foil, shiny side up.

Step 4 Pat the fish to distribute the stuffing evenly.

1. Have the fishmonger gut and bone the fish, leaving on the head and tail. Rinse the fish inside and pat dry.

2. Place the fish on lightly oiled foil. Combine all the stuffing ingredients.

3. Open the cavity of the fish and spoon in the stuffing.

4. Close the fish and pat out gently so that the stuffing is evenly distributed. Close the foil loosely around the fish and place it directly on the oven shelf or in a large roasting pan. Cook at 200°C/400°F/Gas Mark 6 for about 40 minutes. Unwrap the fish and slide it onto a serving plate. Peel off the top layer of skin if desired and garnish with lemon slices.

Cook's Notes

Time
Preparation takes about 25 minutes and cooking takes about 40 minutes.

Preparation
If asked, the fishmonger will gut and bone the fish for you. Fish may also be stuffed with the bone in, but this makes it more difficult to serve.

Variation
Add chopped celery or red or green pepper to the stuffing, if desired.

Chapter V

ENTERTAINING

SERVES 4

HALIBUT AND CRAB HOLLANDAISE

Rich and creamy, the Hollandaise sauce adds an air of sophistication to this lovely dish.

4 large fillets of halibut
1 bay leaf
Slice of onion
5 tbsps white wine
2 egg yolks
1 tbsp lemon juice
Pinch cayenne pepper
Pinch paprika pepper
120g/4oz butter, melted
1 tbsp butter
2 tbsps flour
2 tbsps double cream
Salt and pepper
225g/8oz crab meat

1. Put the fish with the bay leaf, onion slice, wine and just enough water to cover the fish, into a baking dish. Cover and cook in a preheated oven, 160°C/325°F/Gas Mark 3, for 10 minutes.

2. Put the egg yolks, lemon juice, cayenne and paprika into a liquidizer, or food processor. Turn the machine on and gradually pour in the melted butter. Continue processing, until the Hollandaise sauce is thick. Set aside.

3. Put the 1 tbsp unmelted butter into a saucepan, melt over a gentle heat and stir in the flour. Cook gently for 1 minute.

4. Remove the fish from the baking dish and strain the cooking liquor onto the flour and butter in the saucepan,

Step 1 Lay the halibut fillets in an ovenproof dish and poach with the wine, bay leaf, onion slice and just enough water to cover.

Step 2 Add the melted butter very gradually to the egg yolks, lemon juice and seasoning in the liquidizer, to ensure a smooth, thick Hollandaise sauce.

stirring well, to prevent lumps from forming. Cook this sauce gently, until it is smooth and has thickened. Stir in the cream, but do not allow to boil. Season to taste.

5. Stir the crab meat into the fish stock sauce and pour this mixture into a flameproof dish. Lay the halibut fillets on top and cover these with the Hollandaise sauce.

6. Brown under a hot grill before serving.

Cook's Notes

Time
Preparation will take about 15 minutes and cooking takes about 20 minutes.

Preparation
If you do not have a liquidizer or food processor, Hollandaise sauce can be prepared by hand. This should be done by whisking the egg yolks, lemon juice and seasoning in a bowl over a pan of simmering water, then very gradually whisking in the melted butter. This will take about 10 minutes.

Serving Ideas
Serve with new potatoes and broccoli.

SERVES 4

SWORDFISH WITH GRAPEFRUIT SALAD

Rich and dense in texture, swordfish takes very well to
a tart grapefruit accompaniment.

4-6 ruby or pink grapefruit (depending on size)
1 lime
1 spring onion, finely chopped
30ml/2 tbsps chopped fresh coriander or parsley
15g/1 tbsp sugar
4-8 swordfish steaks (depending on size)
Juice of 1 lime
30ml/2 tbsps oil
Black pepper to taste
Coriander sprigs for garnish

1. Remove the zest from the grapefruit and lime with a zester and set it aside.

2. Remove all the pith from the grapefruit and segment them. Mix the grapefruit and citrus zests with the onion, coriander, sugar and lime juice and set aside.

3. Mix remaining lime juice, oil and pepper together and brush both sides of the fish. Place under a pre-heated grill and cook for about 4 minutes each side depending on distance from the heat source.

4. To serve, place a coriander sprig on each fish steak and serve with the grapefruit.

Step 1 Remove the zest from the grapefruit with a zester.

Step 2 Use a serrated fruit knife to remove all the pith from the grapefruit.

Cook's Notes

Time
Preparation takes about 35 minutes and cooking takes about 4-6 minutes.

Preparation
The amount of sugar needed will vary depending on the sweetness of the grapefruit.

Cook's Tip
For extra flavour, the swordfish steaks may be marinated in a lime juice and oil mixture for up to 1 hour.

SERVES 4

SEAFOOD PAN ROAST

This mixture of oysters and crab is a descendant
of French gratin recipes. It's quick to make,
and other seafood may be added.

24 small oysters on the half shell
250ml/9fl oz fish stock
250ml/9fl oz single cream
80g/2½oz butter or margarine
90g/6 tbsps flour
1 bunch spring onions, chopped
50g/2oz parsley, chopped
30ml/2 tbsps Worcester sauce
½ tsp Tabasco
Pinch salt
1 large or 2 small cooked crabs
4 slices bread, crusts trimmed and made into crumbs

Step 3 Turn the crabs over and push out the body with your thumbs.

1. Remove the oysters from their shells with a small, sharp knife. Place the oysters in a saucepan and strain over any oyster liquid. Add the fish stock and cook gently until the oysters curl around the edges. Remove the oysters, keep them warm and strain the liquid into a clean pan.

2. Add the cream to the oyster liquid and bring to the boil. Allow to boil rapidly for about 5 minutes.

3. Remove crab claws and legs. Turn the crabs over and push out the body with your thumbs.

4. Remove the stomach sac and lungs (dead man's fingers) and discard.

5. Cut the body in four sections with a large, sharp knife and pick out the meat with a skewer.

6. Crack claws and legs to extract the meat. Leave the small legs whole for garnish, if desired.

7. Scrape out the brown meat from inside the shell and combine it with the breadcrumbs and white meat from the body and claws.

8. Melt the butter or margarine in a medium-size saucepan and stir in the flour. Cook gently for 5 minutes. Add the onions and parsley and cook a further 5 minutes. Pour over the cream and fish stock mixture, stirring constantly. Add the Worcester sauce, Tabasco and salt, and cook about 15-20 minutes over low heat, stirring occasionally. Fold in the crab meat and breadcrumb mixture.

9. Place the oysters in the bottom of a buttered casserole or in individual dishes and spoon and crab meat mixture on top. Grill to brown, if desired, and serve immediately.

Cook's Notes

Time
Preparation takes about 40 minutes and cooking takes about 30 minutes.

Buying Guide
If fresh oysters on the half shell and freshly cooked crabs are not available, substitute canned oysters and use their liquid for part of the fish stock measurement. Canned oysters will not need as long to cook. Canned or frozen crab meat may be used in place of the fresh crabs, substituting about 8oz for the fresh crab meat.

Serving Ideas
If serving as a first course, this recipe will serve 6. Add French bread and a salad for a light main course.

SERVES 4

SOUR FRIED SEAFOOD

A fragrant sour fried curry from the Far East. This can be served on its own, or as one of a combination of dishes.

1lb mixed fish and seafood, to include any of the
    following: large prawns; scallops; squid, cleaned and
    cut into rings; oysters, shelled; clams, shelled; crab
    claws, shelled; small whole fish, e.g. whitebait or smelt
140ml/¼ pint oil
1 tbsp grated fresh ginger
4 shallots, finely chopped
3 cloves garlic, crushed
4 red chilli peppers, seeded and finely chopped
1 tsp ground mace
½ tsp prawn paste
1 piece tamarind, soaked in 4 tbsps hot water OR
2 tbsps lemon juice
Pinch brown sugar
Salt

Step 1 Fry the fish in hot oil, in several batches, to prevent it from breaking up.

1. Heat the oil in a frying pan, until it begins to smoke. Fry the fish in several batches for 2-3 minutes per batch, or until lightly browned and cooked through. Drain on paper towels and keep warm.

2. Grind the shallots, ginger, garlic, chillies and mace to a smooth paste in a pestle and mortar. Add the prawn paste and blend together well.

3. Put 1 tbsp of oil into a wok and add the spice paste. Cook gently for 2-3 minutes. Strain in the tamarind and

Step 2 Grind the shallots, ginger, garlic, chillies and mace to a smooth paste in a pestle and mortar.

water, or lemon juice. The sauce should be of a thin coating consistency, add a little more water, if it is too thick.

4. Stir in the sugar, the cooked fish and salt to taste. Cook for 2-3 minutes, or until the fish is heated through.

Cook's Notes

Time
Preparation takes about 20 minutes, and cooking takes about 12-15 minutes.

Cook's Tip
Great care should be taken when preparing fresh chillies. Always wash hands thoroughly afterwards, and avoid getting any neat juice in the eyes or mouth. Rinse with copious amounts of clear water, if this happens.

Serving Idea
Serve with a mixed salad, rice and prawn crackers.

SERVES 4

MARINATED TROUT WITH EGG SAUCE

The simply-prepared sauce in this dish allows the flavour of the fish to shine through.

4 even-sized trout, cleaned and trimmed
90ml/6 tbsps red wine
45ml/3 tbsps olive oil
45ml/3 tbsps water
1 clove garlic, crushed
2 sprigs fresh mint, 1 sprig fresh rosemary, 1 sprig fresh thyme, 1 small bay leaf, crumbled
6 black peppercorns
Pinch salt
3 egg yolks, lightly beaten
1 tbsp fresh herbs
Lemon or lime slices to garnish

Step 3 When the fish is cooked, transfer to a serving dish and peel off one side of the skin on each fish.

Step 2 Bring the marinade and fish to the simmering point on top of the stove. Allow to boil.

Step 5 Cook the strained marinade and egg yolks slowly in a double boiler, whisking constantly until the sauce thickens.

1. Place the fish in a roasting pan and pour over the wine, oil, water and add the garlic and herbs. Sprinkle over the peppercorns and the salt and turn the fish several times to coat them thoroughly with the marinade. Leave at room temperature for about 30 minutes.

2. Place the roasting pan with the fish on top of the stove and bring the marinade just to the simmering point. Cover the pan and place in a preheated 180°C/350°F/Gas Mark 4 oven and cook for about 20 minutes or until the fish is firm.

3. Transfer the fish to a serving dish and peel off the skin on one side. Cover and keep warm.

4. Strain the fish cooking liquid into a bowl or the top of a double boiler and discard the herbs and garlic. Mix about 3 tbsps of the liquid into the egg yolks and then return to the bowl or double boiler.

5. Heat slowly, whisking constantly until the sauce thickens. Do not allow the sauce to boil. Add the chopped herbs and adjust the seasoning.

6. Coat the sauce over the skinned side of each trout and garnish the plate with lemon or lime wedges. Serve the rest of the sauce separately.

Cook's Notes

Time
Preparation takes about 30 minutes, cooking takes about 20 minutes for the fish and about 5 minutes to finish the sauce.

Variation
The sauce may be made with white wine instead of red wine if desired.

Serving Ideas
A classic accompaniment is boiled potatoes.

SERVES 6

SZECHUAN FISH

The piquant spiciness of Szechuan pepper is quite different from that of black or white pepper. Beware, though, too much can numb the mouth temporarily!

450g/1lb whitefish fillets
Pinch salt and pepper
1 egg
75g/5 tbsps flour
90ml/6 tbsps white wine
Oil for frying
60g/2oz cooked ham, cut in small dice
2.5cm/1 inch piece fresh ginger, finely diced
½-1 red or green chilli pepper, cored, seeded and finely diced
6 water chestnuts, finely diced
4 spring onions, finely chopped
45ml/3 tbsps light soy sauce
5ml/1 tsp cider vinegar or rice wine vinegar
2.5ml/½ tsp ground Szechuan pepper (optional)
280ml/½ pint light stock
15ml/1 tbsp cornflour dissolved with 30ml/2 tbsps water
10ml/2 tsps sugar

1. To prepare the garnish, choose unblemished chilli peppers with the stems on. Using a small, sharp knife, cut the peppers in strips, starting from the pointed end.

2. Cut down to within 1.25cm/½ inch of the stem end. Rinse out the seeds under cold running water and place the peppers in iced water.

3. Leave the peppers to soak for at least 4 hours or overnight until they open up like flowers.

4. Cut the fish fillets into 5cm/2 inch pieces and season with salt and pepper. Beat the egg well and add flour and wine to make a batter. Dredge the fish lightly with flour and then dip into the batter. Mix the fish well.

5. Heat a wok and when hot, add enough oil to deep-fry the fish. When the oil is hot, fry a few pieces of fish at a time, until golden brown. Drain and proceed until all the fish is cooked.

6. Remove all but 15ml/1 tbsp of oil from the wok and add the ham, ginger, diced chilli pepper, water chestnuts and spring onions. Cook for about 1 minute and add the soy sauce and vinegar. If using Szechuan pepper, add at this point. Stir well and cook for a further 1 minute. Remove the vegetables from the pan and set them aside.

7. Add the stock to the wok and bring to the boil. When boiling, add 1 spoonful of the hot stock to the cornflour mixture. Add the mixture back to the stock and reboil, stirring constantly until thickened.

8. Stir in the sugar and return the fish and vegetables to the sauce. Heat through for 30 seconds and serve at once.

Step 1 Cut the tip of each chilli pepper into strips.

Step 3 Allow to soak 4 hours or overnight to open up.

Cook's Notes

Time
Preparation takes about 30 minutes. Chilli pepper garnish takes at least 4 hours to soak. Cooking takes about 10 minutes.

Serving Ideas
Serve with plain or fried rice. Do not eat the chilli pepper garnish.

Buying Guide
Szechuan peppercorns are available in Chinese supermarkets or delicatessens. If not available, substitute extra chilli pepper.

SERVES 6

KUNG PAO PRAWNS WITH CASHEW NUTS

It is said that Kung Pao invented this dish,
but to this day no one knows who he was!

2.5ml/½ tsp chopped fresh ginger
5ml/1 tsp chopped garlic
25g/1½ tbsps cornflour
1.25ml/¼ tsp bicarbonate of soda
Salt and pepper
1.25ml/¼ tsp sugar
450g/1lb uncooked prawns
60ml/4 tbsps oil
1 small onion, cut into dice
1 large or 2 small courgettes, cut into 1.25cm/½ inch
   cubes
1 small red pepper, cut into 1.25cm/½ inch cubes
60g/2oz cashew nuts

Sauce

180ml/6 fl oz chicken stock
15g/1 tbsp cornflour
10ml/2 tsps chilli sauce
10ml/2 tsps bean paste (optional)
10ml/2 tsps sesame oil
15ml/1 tbsp dry sherry or rice wine

1. Mix together the ginger, garlic, 25g/1½ tbsps cornflour, bicarbonate of soda, salt, pepper and sugar.

2. If the prawns are unpeeled, remove the peels and the dark vein running along the rounded side. If large, cut in half, Place in the dry ingredients and leave to stand for 20 minutes.

3. Heat the oil in a wok and when hot add the prawns. Cook, stirring over high heat for about 20 seconds, or just until the prawns change colour. Transfer to a plate.

4. Add the onion to the same oil in the wok and cook for about 1 minute. Add the courgettes and red pepper and cook about 30 seconds.

5. Mix the sauce ingredients together and add to the wok. Cook, stirring constantly, until the sauce is slightly thickened. Add the prawns and the cashew nuts and heat through completely.

Step 4 To dice the courgettes quickly, top and tail and cut into 1.25cm/½ inch strips.

Step 4 Cut the strips across with a large sharp knife into 1.25cm/½ inch pieces.

Cook's Notes

Time
Preparation takes about 20 minutes, cooking takes about 3 minutes.

Variation
If using cooked prawns, add with the vegetables. Vary amount of chilli sauce to suit your taste.

Serving Ideas
Serve with plain or fried rice.

SERVES 4

SWORDFISH FLORENTINE

Swordfish has an almost "meaty" texture.
Here it has a distinctly Mediterranean flavour.

4 swordfish steaks about 180-225g/6-8oz each in weight
Salt, pepper and lemon juice
Olive oil
900g/2lbs fresh spinach, stems removed and leaves well washed

Garlic Mayonnaise

2 egg yolks
1-2 cloves garlic
Salt, pepper and dry mustard
Pinch cayenne pepper
280ml/½ pint olive oil
Lemon juice or white wine vinegar

1. Sprinkle fish with pepper, lemon juice and olive oil. Place under a pre-heated grill and cook for about 3-4 minutes per side. Fish may also be cooked on an outdoor barbeque grill.

2. Meanwhile, use a sharp knife to shred the spinach finely. Place in a large saucepan and add a pinch of salt. Cover and cook over moderate heat with only the water that clings to the leaves after washing. Cook about 2 minutes, or until leaves are just slightly wilted. Set aside.

3. Place egg yolks in a food processor, blender or cup of a hand blender. Add the garlic, crushed, if using a hand blender. Process several times to mix eggs and purée garlic. Add salt, pepper, mustard and cayenne pepper. With the machine running, pour oil through the funnel in a thin, steady stream. Follow manufacturer's directions if using a hand blender.

4. When the sauce becomes very thick, add some lemon juice or vinegar in small quantities.

5. To serve, place a bed of spinach on a plate and top with the swordfish. Spoon some of the garlic mayonnaise on top of the fish and serve the rest separately.

Step 3 Pour the oil for the sauce onto the egg yolks in a thin, steady stream.

Cook's Notes

Time
Preparation takes about 25 minutes and cooking takes about 6-8 minutes.

Variation
Fresh tuna or halibut may be used in place of the swordfish. Even cod goes well with the sauce and spinach.

Preparation
The garlic mayonnaise may be prepared in advance and will keep for 5-7 days in the refrigerator. It is also delicious served with poached shellfish, chicken or vegetables. If too thick, thin the sauce with hot water.

SERVES 4

SPICED SALMON STEAKS

A blend of spices and sugar makes this easy-to-prepare
salmon dish very out of the ordinary.

120g/4oz light brown sugar
1 tbsp ground allspice
1 tbsp mustard powder
1 tbsp grated fresh ginger
4 salmon steaks, 1 inch thick
1 cucumber
1 bunch spring onions
2 tbsps butter
1 tbsp lemon juice
2 tsps chooped fresh dill weed
1 tbsp chopped fresh parsley
Salt and pepper

1. Mix the sugar and spices together and rub the mixture
into the surface of both sides of the salmon steaks. Allow
the salmon steaks to stand for at least 1 hour in the
refrigerator.

2. Meanwhile prepare the vegetables. Peel the cucumber
and cut into quarters lengthways. Remove the seeds and
cut each quarter into 1 inch pieces.

3. Trim the roots from the spring onions and cut down
some, but not all, of the green part.

4. Put the cucumber and spring onions into a saucepan,
along with the butter, lemon juice, dill, parsley and seasoning. Cook over a moderate heat for about 10 minutes, or
until the cucumber is tender and turning translucent.

5. Put the salmon steaks under a preheated moderate grill
and cook for about 5-6 minutes on each side.

6. Serve with the cucumber and spring onion
accompaniment.

Step 1 Rub the
sugar and spice
mixture into both
surfaces of each
salmon steak.

Step 2 Cut the
peeled cucumber
into quarters
lengthways.
Remove the seeds
and cut each strip
into 1-inch
lengths.

Step 4 Cook the
cucumber and
onion with the
herbs, flavourings,
and butter until the
cucumber is
beginning to
soften and
become
translucent.

Cook's Notes

Time
Preparation takes about 15
minutes, plus standing time of
1 hour, and cooking takes 12-15
minutes.

Preparation
The salmon steaks are ideal for
cooking on an outdoor
barbeque.

Variation
Substitute cod or haddock
steaks for the salmon.

SERVES 4

RED MULLET PROVENÇALE

Red Mullet is a very attractive fish, with a flavour quite
like prawns. It is also known as "woodcock of the sea"
because it is often served with the liver left inside.

30ml/2 tbsps olive oil
1 clove garlic, crushed
2 shallots, finely chopped
450g/1lb ripe tomatoes, peeled, seeded and sliced
10ml/2 tsps chopped marjoram and parsley mixed
90ml/3 fl oz dry white wine
Salt, pepper and pinch saffron
Oil for frying
2 small bulbs fennel, quartered and cored
4 red mullet, about 180g/6oz each
Flour mixed with salt and pepper

1. Heat 30ml/2 tbsps olive oil in a deep saucepan and add
the garlic and shallots. Cook 1-2 minutes to soften slightly,
then add tomatoes, herbs, wine, salt, pepper and saffron.
Allow to simmer, uncovered, for 30 minutes and set aside
while preparing the fennel and fish.

2. Pour about 60ml/4 tbsps oil into a large frying pan or
sauté pan. Place over moderate heat and add the fennel.
Cook quickly until the fennel is slightly browned. Lower the
heat and cook a further 5-10 minutes to soften the fennel.

3. Scale the fish, remove the gills and clean, leaving in the
liver if desired. Wash the fish and dry thoroughly. Trim the
fins and roll the fish in seasoned flour, shaking off the
excess.

4. When the fennel is tender, remove it from the pan and
set it aside. Fry the fish until golden brown on both sides,
about 2-3 minutes per side. Arrange the fish in a warm

Step 3 To scale
fish, run the blunt
end of a knife
from the tail to the
head.

Step 3 Remove
the fins with
kitchen scissors.

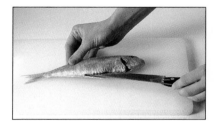

Step 3 Gut the
fish, cut along the
stomach and
remove insides,
leaving liver if
desired.

serving dish and surround with the fennel. Reheat the
sauce and spoon over the fish. Serve remaining sauce
separately.

Cook's Notes

Time
Preparation takes about 30
minutes unless the fish are
already cleaned. Cooking takes
approximately 40 minutes.

Watchpoint
Red mullet spoils quickly, so
use on day of purchase.

Cook's Tip
Saffron is expensive, so use a
pinch of turmeric as a
substitute for colour.

SERVES 6

STUFFED SOLE

Fish is traditionally more popular in Northern Germany than in other parts of the country. This dish is elegant enough for a formal dinner party.

60g/4 tbsps butter or margarine
30g/2 tbsps flour
430ml/¾ pint fish or vegetable stock
90g/3oz button mushrooms, sliced
180g/6oz peeled, cooked prawns
120g/4oz canned, frozen or fresh cooked crabmeat
60ml/4 tbsps double cream
30ml/2 tbsps brandy
30g/1oz fresh breadcrumbs
Salt and pepper
6-12 sole fillets, depending upon size
60g/4 tbsps melted butter

Step 3 Using a filleting knife, begin at the tail end and, using a sawing motion, slide the knife along the skin at a slight angle. Hold the end of the skin tightly with fingers dipped in salt.

Step 3 Spread stuffing on one side of each fillet, and roll up. Secure with cocktail sticks.

Step 3 Cut fillets in half along the natural line that divides them.

1. Preheat the oven to 180°C/350°F/Gas Mark 4. Melt 60g/4 tbsps butter and add the flour. Cook for about 3 minutes over gentle heat or until pale straw coloured. Add the stock and bring to the boil. Add the mushrooms and allow to cook until the sauce thickens.

2. Add the cream and re-boil the sauce. Remove the sauce from the heat and add the brandy, prawns, crab and breadcrumbs.

3. Skin the sole fillets and spread the filling on the side that was skinned. Roll up and arrange in a buttered baking dish. Spoon melted butter over the top and cook in the preheated oven for 20-30 minutes, until the fish is just firm.

Cook's Notes

 Time
Preparation takes about 30 minutes and cooking takes 20-30 minutes.

 Cook's Tip
When skinning fish, dip fingers into salt to get a better grip on slippery fish skin.

 Preparation
Filling may be prepared in advance and covered with a sheet of damp greaseproof paper or clingfilm to prevent a skin from forming on top. Filling is best used when completely cool.

 Serving Ideas
Serve with a green vegetable such as broccoli, asparagus or spinach. Accompany with new potatoes tossed in parsley butter.

 Variation
For special occasions, substitute lobster for the crabmeat for an elegant dinner party.

SERVES 4

MUSSELS À LA GRECQUE

Fresh mussels are a real treat during the autumn and winter
and the sauce in this recipe is a
reminder of warmer days!

1.2 litres/2 pints mussels
1 onion, chopped
120ml/4 fl oz white wine
Lemon juice
2 tbsps olive oil
1 clove garlic, crushed
1 shallot or 2 spring onions, chopped
675g/1½lbs fresh tomatoes, chopped
1 tsp fennel seeds
1 tsp coriander seeds
1 tsp crushed oregano
1 bay leaf
1 tbsp chopped fresh basil
Pinch cayenne pepper
Salt and pepper
Black olives, to garnish

Step 5 Boil the tomato mixture rapidly, until the sauce has reduced and is thick and pulpy.

Step 2 Cook the mussels quickly, until all the shells are open, about 8 minutes. Discard any with shells that stay shut after this time.

1. Scrub the mussels and discard any with broken shells, or which do not shut when tapped with a knife.

2. Put them into a large saucepan with the onion, wine and lemon juice. Cover and cook quickly until the mussels open, discarding any that do not.

3. Remove the mussels from their shells and leave to cool. Reserve the cooking liquid.

4. Heat the olive oil in saucepan and add the garlic and the shallot, or spring onions. Cook gently, until golden brown.

5. Stir in the tomatoes, spices and herbs. Season to taste and blend in the reserved liquor from the mussels. Bring this mixture to the boil and allow to boil rapidly, until the tomatoes are soft and the liquid is reduced by half. Remove the bay leaf.

6. Allow the sauce to cool, then stir in the mussels. Chill well and serve garnished with black olives.

Cook's Notes

Time
Preparation takes about 20 minutes, including cleaning the mussels. Cooking will take about 20 minutes.

Serving Ideas
Serve with a green salad and French bread.

Preparation
The shells of fresh mussels must be tightly closed and intact. Any that are cracked or do not shut tight when tapped with a knife should be thrown away. Any mussels that stay shut after being cooked, should also be discarded.

Cook's Tip
To keep mussels fresh overnight, wrap them in a thick layer of damp newspaper. Put this inside a polythene bag and store them in the bottom of a refrigerator. DO NOT KEEP FRESH SHELLFISH FOR ANY LONGER THAN OVERNIGHT.

SERVES 4

MONKFISH AND PEPPER KEBABS WITH BEARNAISE BUTTER SAUCE

Monkfish is a firm, succulent whitefish, ideal for kebabs.

8 strips bacon, boned and rind removed
2 pieces lemon grass
900g/2lbs monkfish, cut into 2-inch pieces
1 green pepper, seeded and cut into 2-inch pieces
1 red pepper, seeded and cut into 2-inch pieces
12 button mushrooms, washed and trimmed
8 bay leaves
Oil for brushing
120ml/4 fl oz dry white wine
4 tbsps tarragon vinegar
2 shallots, finely chopped
1 tbsp chopped fresh tarragon
1 tbsp chopped fresh chervil or parsley
225g/8oz butter, melted
Salt and pepper

1. Cut the bacon in half lengthways and then in half across. Peel the lemon grass and use only the core. Cut this into small shreds.

2. Place a piece of fish on each strip of bacon and top with a shred of lemon grass. Roll up the bacon around the fish. Thread each fish and bacon roll onto kebab skewers, alternating with the pepper, mushrooms and bay leaves. Brush well with oil.

3. Cook under a moderate grill for 15 minutes, turning frequently and brushing with more oil, if necessary, until the fish is cooked.

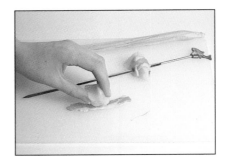

Step 2 Place a piece of fish onto a strip of bacon and top with a shred of lemon grass. Roll and thread onto kebab skewers.

Step 5 Stir the herbs into the reduced wine mixture. Lower the heat and beat in the butter, bit by bit, until the sauce is thick and creamy.

4. Heat together the wine, vinegar and shallots in a small saucepan until they are boiling. Cook rapidly until reduced by half.

5. Stir in the herbs and lower the heat. Beat in the butter, a little at a time, until the sauce is the thickness of an Hollandaise. Season to taste and serve with the kebabs.

Cook's Notes

 Time Preparation takes about 30 minutes, and cooking takes about 25 minutes.

 Preparation These kebabs are ideal for cooking over a barbecue.

 Serving Ideas Serve with a large mixed salad and rice, or pasta.

234

SERVES 2-3

DRESSED CRAB

No book on fish cookery would be complete without instructions on how to dress a crab. Do not buy a crab which sounds to have water in when shaken.

1 large cooked crab
Chopped fresh parsley, to garnish

Step 2 Lay the crab on its upper shell and pull the underbody firmly away from the main shell.

1. Pull off the crab claws, and crack these with a small hammer or nutcrackers. Pull out the meat and put into a basin for light meat.

2. Turn the crab onto its back or uppermost shell, and pull the underbody firmly away from the main shell.

3. Remove and discard the stomach bag and grey, feathered gills, or fingers, as these must not be eaten. Scoop out the dark meat from the shell with a spoon and put into a basin.

4. Crack open the underbody and remove all the white meat with a skewer or fork. Put into the appropriate basin.

Step 3 Remove and discard the stomach bag which lies behind the head, and the grey, finger-like gills, as these must never be eaten.

Step 5 Carefully crack away enough of the edges of the upper shell to form a flat case, in which to serve the crab meat.

5. Remove enough of the top shell to make a flat case, in which to serve the meat. Scrub the shell thoroughly.

6. Arrange layers of dark and light meat alternately in the shell, and garnish with the parsley.

Cook's Notes

Time
Preparation takes about 35-45 minutes.

Serving Ideas
Serve with new potatoes and a simple, mixed lettuce salad.

Cook's Tip
Use fresh crabs on the same day that you purchase them. Always buy them from a reputable source. If you must store them until the next day, wrap them in damp newspaper and keep them in the bottom of a refrigerator.

Variation
To make the crab serve 4 people, hard-boil 2 eggs, chop the whites and sieve the yolks and arrange these in stripes with the dark and light crab meat.

SERVES 4

RED MULLET WITH HERB AND MUSHROOM SAUCE

This is a Mediterranean fish with a slight taste of prawns.
It is often cooked with the liver left in − a delicacy.

450g/1lb small mushrooms, left whole
1 clove garlic, finely chopped
45ml/3 tbsps olive oil
Juice of 1 lemon
15ml/1 tbsp finely chopped parsley
10ml/2 tsps finely chopped basil
5ml/1 tsp finely chopped marjoram or sage
60ml/4 tbsps dry white wine mixed with 2.5ml/½ tsp
   cornflour
Few drops anchovy essence
4 red mullet, each weighing about 225g/8oz
10ml/2 tsps white breadcrumbs
10ml/2 tsps freshly grated Parmesan cheese

1. Combine the mushrooms, garlic and olive oil in a small frying pan. Cook over moderate heat for about 1 minute, until the garlic and mushrooms are slightly softened. Add all the herbs, lemon juice and white wine and cornflour mixture. Bring to the boil and cook until thickened. Add anchovy essence to taste. Set aside while preparing the fish.

2. To clean the fish, cut along the stomach from the gills to the vent, the small hole near the tail. Clean out the cavity of the fish, leaving the liver, if desired.

3. To remove the gills, lift the flap and snip them out with a sharp pair of scissors. Rinse the fish well and pat dry.

4. Place the fish head to tail in a shallow ovenproof dish that can be used for serving. The fish should fit snugly into the dish.

5. Pour the prepared sauce over the fish and sprinkle with the breadcrumbs and Parmesan cheese.

6. Cover the dish loosely with foil and cook in the preheated oven 190°C/375°F/Gas Mark 5, for about 20 minutes. Uncover for the last 5 minutes, if desired, and raise the oven temperature slightly. This will lightly brown the fish.

Step 3 Lift the flap over the gills and use kitchen scissors to snip the gills away.

Step 4 Place the fish head to tail in a shallow baking dish just large enough to accommodate them.

Cook's Notes

Time
Preparation takes about 30 minutes, cooking takes about 5 minutes for the sauce and 20 minutes for the fish.

Preparation
If the fish need to be scaled, use the blunt edge of a knife and scrape from the tail to the head. Rinse well and remove any loose scales. The fishmonger will gut the fish, scale them and remove the gills if desired.

Variations
Use other fish such as bream or sardines.

SERVES 4

GRILLED FISH

Grilling fish with herbs and lemon is one of the most delightful ways of preparing it, and is particularly common in the Greek Islands.

2 large bream or other whole fish
Fresh thyme and oregano
Olive oil
Lemon juice
Salt and pepper
Lemon wedges
Vine leaves

1. Preheat a grill. Gut the fish and rinse it well. Pat dry and sprinkle the cavity with salt, pepper and lemon juice. Place sprigs of herbs inside.

2. Make 3 diagonal cuts on the sides of the fish with a sharp knife. Place the fish on the grill rack and sprinkle with olive oil and lemon juice.

3. Cook on both sides until golden brown and crisp. This should take about 8-10 minutes per side, depending on the thickness of the fish.

To make perfect lemon wedges, first cut the ends off the lemons, then cut in 4 or 8 wedges and remove the membrane and seeds.

Step 1 Open the cavity of the fish and sprinkle with salt, pepper and lemon juice.

Step 2 Use a sharp knife to make diagonal cuts on both sides of each fish.

4. If using vine leaves preserved in brine, rinse them well. If using fresh vine leaves, pour over boiling water and leave to stand for about 10 minutes to soften slightly. Drain and allow to cool. Line a large serving platter with the vine leaves and when the fish is cooked place it on top of the leaves. Serve surrounded with lemon wedges.

Cook's Notes

 Time
Preparation takes about 20 minutes, cooking takes about 16-20 minutes, depending upon the size of the fish.

 Cook's Tip
When grilling large whole fish, slit the skin on both sides to help the fish cook evenly.

 Variation
The fish may be wrapped in vine leaves before grilling. This keeps the fish moist and adds extra flavour. Other fish suitable for cooking by this method are red mullet, trout, sea bass, grey mullet, sardines, herring or mackerel.

 Preparation
If desired, the fish may be cooked on an outdoor barbecue grill. Wait until the coals have white ash on the top and be sure to oil the racks before placing on the fish, or use a special wire cage for cooking fish.

SERVES 4
PAN FRIED TROUT

Trout is so delicious that simple preparation
is all that's necessary. Crisp cornmeal, bacon and
pine nuts complement the fresh flavour.

90-120ml/3-4 fl oz vegetable oil
60g/4 tbsps pine nuts
8 rashers streaky bacon, diced
140g/4 oz yellow cornmeal
Pinch salt and white pepper
4 trout weighing about 225g/8oz each, cleaned
Juice of 1 lime
Fresh sage or coriander

1. Heat 90ml/6 tbsps of the oil in a large frying pan. Add the pine nuts and cook over moderate heat, stirring constantly. When a pale golden brown, remove them with a draining spoon to paper towels.

2. Add the diced bacon to the oil and cook until crisp, stirring constantly. Drain with the pine nuts.

3. Mix the cornmeal, salt and pepper, and dredge the fish well, patting on the cornmeal. Shake off any excess.

4. If necessary, add more oil to the pan – it should come about halfway up the sides of the fish. Re-heat over moderately high heat.

5. When hot, add the fish two at a time and fry until golden brown, about 4-5 minutes. Turn over and reduce the heat slightly if necessary and cook a further 4-5 minutes. Drain and repeat with the remaining fish.

6. Drain almost all the oil from the pan and re-heat the bacon and the nuts very briefly. Add the lime juice and cook a few seconds. Spoon the bacon and pine nut mixture over the fish and garnish with coriander or sage.

Step 3 Dredge the fish with the cornmeal mixture, shaking off any excess.

Step 5 Place the fish two at a time in hot oil and fry until golden brown on one side, then turn.

Step 6 Spoon the bacon, pine nut and lime juice mixture over the fish.

Cook's Notes

Time
Preparation takes about 25 minutes and cooking takes about 15-20 minutes.

Preparation
When coating fish, seafood or chicken for frying, prepare just before ready to cook. If the food stands with its coating for too long before cooking, the coating will become soggy.

Variation
If desired, the trout may be dredged with plain or wholemeal flour instead of the cornmeal.

SERVES 4

BAKED RED MULLET WITH GARLIC AND TOMATOES

This is a fish that appears often in Mediterranean cookery.

4 even-sized red mullet
45ml/3 tbsps olive oil
45ml/3 tbsps dry white wine
1 lemon
2 cloves garlic, crushed
Salt and pepper
340g/12oz fresh tomatoes, thinly sliced or 400g/14oz
    canned tomatoes, strained
Sprigs of fresh dill for garnish

1. Preheat the oven to 190°C/375°F/Gas Mark 5. First scale the fish by running the blunt edge of a large knife over the skin of the fish going from the tail to the head.

2. Using a filleting knife, cut along the belly of the fish from just under the head to the vent, the small opening near the tail. Clean out the cavity of the fish, leaving in the liver if desired. Rinse the fish well inside and out and pat dry.

Step 1 To scale the fish, hold it by the tail and run the blunt side of a knife down the length of the body from the tail to the head.

Step 2 To gut the fish, cut with a filleting knife from just under the head to the vent and remove the insides of the fish.

Step 3 Rinse the fish well under cold running water and, using kitchen scissors, trim the tail and fins.

3. Trim the fins and neaten the tail with kitchen scissors. Place the fish head to tail in an ovenproof dish. Mix the oil and the wine together and squeeze the juice from one of the lemons. Add the garlic, salt and pepper and pour over the fish. Place on the tomato slices or if using canned tomatoes, crush them slightly and spoon over. Bake for about 25 minutes, basting frequently until the fish is tender. Garnish with dill.

Cook's Notes

Variation
Add thinly sliced fennel to the fish before baking, in addition to the tomatoes. Substitute other fish such as sea bass, grey mullet, or fish steaks such as cod or halibut.

Time
Preparation takes about 20 minutes, cooking takes about 25 minutes.

Cook's Tip
Red mullet spoils quickly, so use on the day of purchase.

SERVES 2

SWEET-SOUR FISH

In China this dish is almost always
prepared with freshwater fish, but
sea bass is also an excellent choice.

1 sea bass, grey mullet or carp, weighing about
    900g/2lbs, cleaned
15ml/1 tbsp dry sherry
Few slices fresh ginger
120g/4oz sugar
90ml/6 tbsps cider vinegar
15ml/1 tbsp soy sauce
30g/2 tbsps cornflour
1 clove garlic, crushed
2 spring onions, shredded
1 small carrot, peeled and finely shredded
30g/1oz bamboo shoots, shredded

1. Rinse the fish well inside and out. Make three diagonal cuts on each side of the fish with a sharp knife.

2. Trim off the fins, leaving the dorsal fin on top.

3. Trim the tail to two neat points.

4. Bring enough water to cover the fish to the boil in a wok. Gently lower the fish into the boiling water and add the sherry and ginger. Cover the wok tightly and remove at once from the heat. Allow to stand 15-20 minutes to let the fish cook in the residual heat.

5. To test if the fish is cooked, pull the dorsal fin – if it comes off easily the fish is done. If not, return the wok to the heat and bring to the boil. Remove from the heat and leave the fish to stand a further 5 minutes. Transfer the fish to a heated serving dish and keep it warm. Take all but 60ml/4 tbsps of the fish cooking liquid from the wok. Add the remaining ingredients including the vegetables and cook, stirring constantly, until the sauce thickens. Spoon some of the sauce over the fish to serve and serve the rest separately.

Step 1 Rinse the fish well and make three diagonal cuts on each side.

Step 2 Using kitchen scissors, trim all of the fins except the dorsal fin at the top.

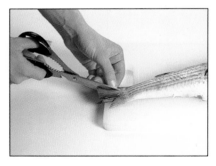

Step 3 Using kitchen scissors again, trim the ends of the tail to two sharp points.

Cook's Notes

Time
Preparation takes about 25 minutes, cooking takes about 15-25 minutes.

Cook's Tip
The diagonal cuts in the side of the fish ensure even cooking.

Variation
If desired, use smaller fish such as trout or red mullet and shorten the cooking time to 10-15 minutes.

Preparation
The fish may also be cooked in the oven in a large roasting pan or in greased foil sprinkled with sherry. Cook at 190°C/375°F/Gas Mark 5 for 10 minutes per 1.25cm/½ inch thickness, measured around the middle of the fish.

SERVES 4

STUFFED TROUT WITH YOGURT SAUCE

1 boned trout, (about 900g/2lb in boned weight)
225g/8oz ham
Water
1 small green pepper, seeded and finely chopped
2 small onions, finely chopped
1 slice bread, made into crumbs
60ml/4 tbsps lemon juice
Lemon juice
140ml/¼ pint natural yogurt
5ml/1 tsp garlic powder
10ml/2 tsps chopped coriander
Salt and pepper

1. Have the fishmonger bone the trout, leaving the head and tail on the fish.

2. Combine ham with the green pepper, onion, breadcrumbs and lemon juice.

3. Sprinkle the fish cavity with salt and pepper.

4. Stuff the fish with the sausage mixture and place on lightly-oiled foil. Seal the ends to form a parcel and bake in a pre-heated 180°C/350°F/Gas Mark 4 oven for about 20-30 minutes, or until the fish feels firm and the flesh looks opaque.

5. Combine the yogurt, garlic powder, coriander and seasonings to taste.

6. Remove the fish from the foil and transfer to a serving plate. Spoon some of the sauce over the fish and serve the rest separately.

Step 3 Sprinkle the fish cavity with lemon juice.

Step 4 When the stuffing ingredients are well mixed, spoon into the fish on one half and press the other half down lightly to spread the stuffing evenly.

Step 4 Seal the foil loosely around the fish.

Cook's Notes

Time
Preparation takes about 25 minutes and cooking takes about 10 minutes for pre-cooking the sausage and 25 minutes for cooking the fish.

Serving Ideas
A classic accompaniment is boiled potatoes.

Variation
Other whole fish such as sea bass or grey mullet may be used with the stuffing, however, the stuffing doesn't compliment salmon.

SERVES 4-6

STUFFED FISH

A whole baked fish makes an impressive main course
for a dinner party. The stuffing makes the fish go
further and with no bones it's easy to serve and eat.

900g-1.5kg/2-3lb whole fish such as carp, sea bass or
    salmon trout
30g/2 tbsps melted butter

Stuffing

15g/1 tbsp butter or margarine
1 small onion, finely chopped
120g/4oz mushrooms, roughly chopped
1 hard-boiled egg, peeled and roughly chopped
90g/3oz fresh breadcrumbs, white or wholemeal
Pinch salt and pepper
10ml/2 tsps chopped fresh dill
10ml/2 tsps chopped fresh parsley
Pinch nutmeg

Sauce

140ml/¼ pint sour cream
Pinch sugar
Grated rind and juice of ½ lemon
Pinch salt and white pepper
Lemon slices and parsley sprigs to garnish

1. Ask the fishmonger to gut and bone the fish for you,
leaving on the head and tail. Sprinkle the cavity of the fish
with salt and pepper and set it aside while preparing the
stuffing.

2. To chop the onion finely, peel it and cut it in half lengthways. Place the onion cut side down on a chopping board.
Using a large, sharp knife, make four cuts into the onion,
parallel to the chopping board, but not completely through

Step 2 Slice the
onion crosswise
into individual
dice.

to the root end. Using the pointed tip of the knife, make four
or five cuts into the onion lengthways, following the natural
lines in the onion and not cutting through to the root end.
Next, cut the onion crossways into thin or thick slices as
desired and the onion should fall apart into individual dice.
Keep fingers well out of the way when slicing.

3. Melt the butter or margarine in a medium-sized saucepan and add the chopped onion and mushrooms. Cook
briefly to soften the vegetables and set aside. Stir in the
remaining stuffing ingredients.

4. Spread the stuffing evenly into the cavity of the fish and
place the fish in lightly buttered foil or in a large baking dish.
Sprinkle the top with melted butter and bake in a preheated
180°C/350°F/Gas Mark 4 oven for about 40 minutes,
basting frequently. If the fish begins to dry out too much on
top, cover loosely with the foil.

5. When the fish is cooked, combine the sauce ingredients and pour over the fish. Cook a further 5 minutes to heat
the sauce, but do not allow it to bubble. Remove the fish to
a serving dish and garnish with lemon and parsley.

Cook's Notes

Cook's Tip
Cover the head and tail of the
fish with lightly greased foil
about halfway through cooking time .
This will prevent the fish from drying out
and improve the appearance of the
finished dish.

Time
Preparation takes about 20
minutes. If boning the fish
yourself, add a further 30 minutes.
Cooking takes approximately 45
minutes.

Variation
Other vegetables, such as
grated carrot, finely chopped
green or red pepper or peeled, seeded
and chopped tomatoes may be added
to the stuffing.

SERVES 4

TROUT IN ASPIC

A dish using crystal-clear aspic is always
impressive, and home-made aspic has a flavour
that is well worth the effort to make.

1.5 litres/3 pints water
Pinch salt and 6 black peppercorns
2 bay leaves and 2 parsley stalks
1 small onion, diced
280ml/½ pint dry white wine
4 even-sized rainbow trout, gutted and well washed
2 egg whites
30g/2 level tbsps powdered gelatine
Lemon slices, capers and sprigs of fresh dill for garnish

Step 9 Decorate the top of the fish and set with a bit of aspic. When firm, cover the trout with the remaining aspic.

1. Combine the water, vinegar, salt, peppercorns, bay leaves, parsley stalks, sliced onion and wine in a large saucepan or fish kettle. Bring to the boil and allow to simmer for about 30 minutes.

2. Cool slightly and add the fish. Cover and bring back to the simmering point. Allow the fish to cook gently for 5 minutes. Cool in the liquid, uncovered, until lukewarm.

3. Carefully remove the fish, drain and peel the skin off both sides while the fish is still slightly warm. Strain the liquid and reserve it.

4. Carefully lift the fillets from both sides of the trout, taking care not to break them up. Make sure they are completely free of skin and bones and place them on individual plates, or onto one large serving plate that has a slight well in the centre.

5. Pour the reserved fish cooking liquid into a large, deep saucepan and add the egg whites. Place the pan over the heat and whisk by hand using a wire balloon whisk. Allow the mixture to come to the boil, whisking constantly. Egg whites should form a thick frothy crust on top.

6. Stop whisking and allow the liquid and egg whites to boil up the side of the pan. Take off the heat and allow to subside. Repeat the process twice more and then leave to settle.

7. Line a colander with several thicknesses of paper towels or a clean tea towel. Place in a bowl and pour the fish cooking liquid and the egg white into the colander. Leave to drain slowly. Do not allow the egg white to fall into the clarified liquid.

8. When all the liquid has drained through, remove about 280ml/½ pint and dissolve the gelatine in it. Heat again very gently if necessary to dissolve the gelatine thoroughly. Return the gelatine to the remaining stock, place the bowl in a bowl of ice water to help thicken the gelatine.

9. Decorate the trout and the base of the dish with lemon slices, capers and fresh dill. When the aspic has become syrupy and slightly thickened, spoon carefully over the decoration to set it. Place in the refrigerator until set.

10. The aspic may be reheated gently by placing the bowl in a pan of hot water. Do not stir the aspic too vigorously or bubbles will form. Chill again until almost set and cover the trout completely in a layer of aspic. Place in the refrigerator until completely set and serve cold.

Cook's Notes

Time
Preparation takes about 40 minutes to 1 hour. Cooking time for the trout is about 35 minutes. The aspic takes about 15 minutes to clarify.

Preparation
Adding egg whites to a stock removes any sediment that makes the stock cloudy. The sediment remains in the egg whites, hence it is important not to let the crust fall back into the clarified stock.

Cook's Tip
If the aspic is still cloudy after straining, pour back through the colander and the egg white crust into a clean bowl. This usually produces a very clear aspic.

SERVES 4

FISH PARCELS

A famous New Orleans dish that cannot fail to impress at a special dinner party, this recipe demands the use of freshly prepared fish stock.

8 single or 4 double whitefish fillets
Fishbones and trimmings
1 bay leaf, sprig thyme and 2 parsley stalks
6 black peppercorns
1 slice lemon
250ml/9fl oz dry white wine
250ml/9fl oz water
8 large uncooked prawns, shelled
4 crab claws, cracked and shelled
60g/2oz butter or margarine
45g/3 tbsps flour
1 onion, finely chopped
Pinch salt and pepper
2 egg yolks

1. Preheat the oven to 200°C/400°F/Gas Mark 6. To make fish stock, skin the fish fillets and place the skin in a large stockpot along with the fish bones, thyme, bay leaf, peppercorns and lemon slice. Add the wine and water and bring to the boil. Lower the heat and simmer for 20 minutes. Strain and set aside.

2. Cut wax paper or baking parchment into large ovals big enough to form a parcel for each fish fillet. Fold the paper in half and lightly oil both sides.

3. Place the fish fillets on one half of the paper and arrange the prawn and crab claws on top of each fillet.

4. Melt the butter in a heavy-based saucepan and, when foaming, add the flour. Cook over moderate heat for 2-3 minutes, stirring frequently until a pale straw colour. Add the onion and cook until lightly browned.

5. Gradually pour on the fish stock, whisking continuously. Cook over moderate heat for about 4-5

Step 3 Place the fish fillets, prawn and crab claws on the greased paper.

Step 6 Spoon the prepared sauce over the fish.

minutes, or until the sauce thickens.

6. Mix the egg yolks with a few spoonfuls of the hot sauce and then stir the egg yolks into the sauce. Spoon some of the sauce over each fillet and seal the parcels, folding the edge over twice and twisting the ends slightly to seal completely.

7. Place the parcels on baking sheets or in shallow baking pans and place in the preheated oven for about 20 minutes.

8. Serve the parcels unopened, to be opened at the table. Serve any remaining sauce separately.

Cook's Notes

Time
Preparation takes about 40 minutes. Cooking takes about 20 minutes for the stock, 7-8 minutes for the sauce and 20 minutes to finish the dish.

Cook's Tip
When making fish stock, cook for only 20 minutes with the fishbones in. Overcooking will result in a bitter tasting stock.

Preparation
If reheating extra sauce to serve, place over gentle heat and stir constantly until heated through. Do no allow the sauce to boil or the sauce will curdle.

INDEX